Rabies and wildlife

Frontispiece: A radio-tagged fox showing almost as much opportunism as the people with whom it cohabits. (Photograph courtesy of N. G. Hough.)

RABIES AND WILDLIFE

a biologist's perspective

DAVID W. MACDONALD

1980

OXFORD UNIVERSITY PRESS

EARTH RESOURCES RESEARCH LIMITED

Oxford University Press, Walton Street, Oxford OX2 6DP

OXFORD   LONDON   GLASGOW
NEW YORK   TORONTO   MELBOURNE   WELLINGTON
KUALA LUMPUR   SINGAPORE   JAKARTA   HONG KONG   TOKYO
DELHI   BOMBAY   CALCUTTA   MADRAS   KARACHI
NAIROBI   DAR ES SALAAM   CAPE TOWN

Earth Resources Research Ltd
40 James Street, London W.1

© Earth Resources Research Ltd 1980

Published in the USA by Oxford University Press, New York

British Library Cataloguing in Publication Data

Macdonald, David W
    Rabies and wildlife.
    1. Rabies
    I. Title II. Earth Resources Research
    616.9′53   RC148   79-41391

    ISBN 0-19-857567-X
    ISBN 0-19-857576-9 Pbk

Lowe & Brydone Printers Ltd, Thetford, Norfolk

Preface

Throughout much of the world wildlife is threatened, either directly or indirectly, through habitat destruction. Sometimes man's behaviour towards other species stems from greed, thoughtlessness, or prejudice. In other cases there is real conflict between our interests and those of wildlife; it is in these areas that we must strive for a better understanding of animals so that we can resolve genuine wildlife problems without unnecessary ecological imbalance. There can be few more vivid or complex issues facing the wildlife biologist than the control of rabies. In this book I have not attempted a complete review of knowledge concerning rabies; Nagano and Davenport (1971), Bisseru (1972), and the excellent volumes edited by Baer (1975) have already achieved this. Neither have I attempted an exhaustive review of every aspect of the biology of foxes or any other vector of the disease. Rather, I have written about those topics where knowledge, or more interestingly ignorance, highlights the biological problems involved in rabies control. It would be foolhardy to propose a definitive solution to any wildlife problem, and I have certainly not done so here. I do argue, however, for a method of thinking about rabies control which takes into account the intricate relationships between a species' ecological circumstances and its behaviour and acknowledges the enthralling subtlety of animal behaviour and natural communities.

Part of the fun of writing this book has been the opportunity to meet and talk with specialists in diverse fields. Many people have read parts of the book and suggested helpful changes, often generously on the basis of unpublished material. In this respect I am grateful to Dr L. Andral (Centre National d'Études sur la Rage, France), Professor P. Armitage and Mr F. Ball (Biomathematics Department, Oxford), Mr P. Bacon and Dr H. Kruuk (Institute of Terrestrial Ecology, U.K.), Dr G. Baer (Centre for Disease Control, Georgia), Dr. C. R. O. Everard (Medical Research Council, Grenada), Professor C. Kaplan (Virology Department, Reading), Mr H. G. Lloyd (Ministry of Agriculture, Fisheries, and Food, U.K.), Dr D. Mollison (Department of Actuarial Mathematics and Statistics, Herriot Watt University, Edinburgh), and Dr D. Warrel (Radcliffe Infirmary, Oxford). I am especially in debt to Dr George Baer for his help and infectious enthusiasm and to Graham Searle of Earth Resources Research Ltd for encouraging me to write this book.

Balliol College, Oxford   D. W. M.
May 1979

For my father

Dr W. A. F. Macdonald

Contents

1 The background

Government posters proclaiming the appalling consequences of the possible arrival of rabies, *la rage, la rabia,* or *der Tollwut* on British shores greet all travellers at every point of entry to the United Kingdom. Indeed, an official campaign to alert the British public to the possible dangers of rabies and a resulting alarmist echo from the media have, in combination, had the result that most of the British public have not only heard of rabies, but are afraid of it. In contrast, many travellers from countries where rabies is presently endemic frown quizzically at these warning posters and ask what all the fuss is about.

In this book I shall try to answer that question through consideration of what is known about the disease rabies as a threat to human life, domestic stock, and wildlife. In many regions rabies is spread by wildlife, usually with one dominant vector species in each area. Schemes to halt the spread of the disease frequently constitute a battle against these wild vectors. In Europe at the time of writing the wild animal most seriously implicated in the spread of rabies is the red fox, *Vulpes vulpes,* and should rabies infect wildlife in Britain it will probably be the fox that poses the most serious problem.

As a biologist, I believe that the epizootiology† of rabies can best be understood through a thorough knowledge of the behaviour of its vectors (e.g. the fox), and its control and prevention can most fruitfully be tackled from an understanding of the behavioural and ecological factors involved. So, after describing first the prevailing distribution of rabies, I shall try to explore how this may relate to our knowledge of fox biology and, most important of all, to consider solutions to the problem which are not only effective, but which also minimize ecological disruption.

Rabies (the Latin origin of this word is derived from the Sanskrit *rabhar,* to do violence) is only one of many problems causing conflict between man and wildlife. Until recently we have either not had, or have ignored, knowledge to enable such problems to be tackled objectively while striving for the minimum imbalance for the environment, or ecosystem. In fact, the practical solution to almost every wildlife problem has been straightforward—slaughter. Nowadays the tide of opinion is changing in favour of thoughtful conservation and management; moreover, new discoveries by researchers in animal behaviour and ecology reveal that wars with nature may not only be undesirable,

† The study of the spread of disease in animal populations; from the Greek *epi* (= upon) and *zōios* (= animal).

but also counterproductive. In the name of rabies control hundreds of thousands of carnivores have been killed in different regions of the world; at enormous cost, both to taxpayers and environment. In spite of these efforts the disease has generally continued to spread. For this reason it is necessary to review from a biologist's standpoint the thinking behind these schemes and to consider whether alternatives exist which are equally or more efficient while being cheaper, either in lives or money.

Men began recording their fear of rabies more than two thousand years ago. Symptoms which probably resulted from rabies were considered by the ancient civilizations of the Nile and Euphrates to be punishment for eating illicit food or to reflect prevailing weather conditions. Acteon, a mythical hunter, surprised Diana while bathing and in consequence was torn apart by a pack of supposedly rabid dogs. Homer claims that Sirius, the dog star, exerts an evil influence on man, and Steele (1975) believes this refers to rabies. The idea of rabies being a contagious disease transmitted by biting animals was certainly familiar to Aristotle and was mentioned by Hippocrates in the fourth and fifth centuries B.C. (Steele 1973). Interestingly, Aristotle maintained that while mad dogs infected other animals with their bites, they did not apparently infect man; another surprising aspect of ancient writings is that ninth-century Byzantine authors thought rabies to be a curable disease.

Records from the Middle Ages show that rabies was then widespread in Europe and also in Britain. For the most part references are to madness in dogs, as these pose the greatest threat in terms of human infection. However, in the twelfth century and thereafter there are references to several species of wildlife which are implicated in the spread of the disease. These include foxes and badgers together with other species such as bears and wolves whose range has more recently been drastically reduced through persecution by man. Indeed it appears that the wolf epitomized the most fearsome of rabid wild animals in the minds of people of the Middle Ages. For a wolf to attack humans is almost unheard of today and study of old research suggests that most of the supposedly ferocious wolves of the past were probably rabid. For instance, at Hue-An-Gal in France a rabid wolf bit 46 people in one day during 1851.

Epidemic diseases like rabies often occur in cycles. After one major European outbreak in the sixteenth century, another is recorded as beginning early in the eighteenth century. Britain was also affected at this time and by the middle of the eighteenth century many rabid dogs had been reported in London.

In spite of sporadic mention of wild animals, in particular foxes and wolves, during these early epidemics (or epizootics as they are called when referring to outbreaks of disease in animal populations) the emphasis remained clearly on the effects of the disease, whether on humans or on domestic animals, particularly dogs. This view changed, at least in Europe, during an outbreak following the Napoleonic Wars. At that time foxes were so heavily infected with the disease that, as Steele (1975) has noted, 'the involvement of foxes obtruded on to the senses of even the dimmest observer' (see also Kaplan 1977). Not only were numerous foxes found dying or dead from rabies, but around the Jura Mountains in particular, livestock and people were attacked and bitten. Between 1800 and 1835 the epizootic spread across Switzerland. Furthermore, it penetrated Germany, reaching Bavaria by 1820 and the Black Forest by 1825. In the other direction the disease was infecting Hesse by the mid-1820s. Kaplan points out the similarity in the regions infected during the post-Napoleonic outbreak to those infected during our present epizooty in the 1970s. He also stresses an important difference; namely, the reputed savagery of foxes during this nineteenth-century epizootic, which is not observed today. Steele (1975) has written an interesting and comprehensive account of the history of rabies.

Nowadays people in Britain often imagine that because the country is free from rabies, it has always been so. Actually, as mentioned earlier, there was rabies in Britain throughout much of recorded history, the earliest mention being in the laws of Howel the Good, of Wales in 1026. The British Isles share this recent freedom from the disease with several other countries where it was also once endemic; for example, Sweden and Norway eradicated it in the mid-nineteenth century. Some of the best records of rabies in Britain are to be found in hunting literature. Authors in the fifteenth century were clearly aware of the risk to their prized hounds from bites from infected animals, but references to rabid wild animals in Britain are scarce. Indeed it is difficult to be certain whether, for example, British foxes have ever been implicated in a rabies epidemic. Admittedly, Edward, Second Duke of York, alluded to wolves becoming mad and thereafter biting men who subsequently died (which was attributed to a venom derived from the wolves' supposed habit of eating toads). But, as Lloyd (1976) points out, it is possible that Edward's statement refers to observations made in France. Kaplan (1977) concludes that British carnivores have never been implicated in rabies transmission, although two physicians mention human cases following fox bites. One of these (Mead in 1708) records a fox being bitten by a mad dog and subsequently biting his patient. The circumstances of these cases remain uncertain and the reason for the absence or sporadic incidence of fox-borne rabies in Britain during historic times presents an interesting problem. In Britain in the 1750s rabies was sufficiently serious for two shillings to be offered for each mad dog killed.

Twenty years later paupers were not allowed to keep dogs, as a way of reducing the number of dogs.

The later nineteenth century appears to have witnessed the most serious outbreaks in Britain, with London and Lancashire being foci for the disease. In 1864 one thousand stray dogs were killed in Liverpool in an attempt to destroy rabid animals. In 1866, 36 people died from rabies, of whom 13 were Lancashire men and 11 Londoners. This led in 1867 to the Metropolitan Streets Act which empowered the police to capture vagrant dogs. While this Act helped to contain the disease in London rabies spread in the north of England from Lancashire into Yorkshire and also north into Scotland. Published reports relate almost entirely to the involvement of dogs in the spread; for instance, the famous account by Fleming in 1872 tells of a rabid retriever which had been infected near Wigan and in the ensuing month travelled through Derby, Nottingham, and Loughborough, biting several people *en route*. Kaplan (1977) points out that if this report is accurate the rabid animal had covered at least a hundred miles. Similarly, Barclay (1958) reports that a rabid clumber spaniel travelled more than fifty miles in 24 hours in Norfolk. This spaniel bit at least ten people.

Rabies control remained an issue tackled locally and the disease thus continued to spread. In 1874, 74 people died from rabies in Britain and continuing deaths led to the Rabies Order of 1877, which empowered parish magistrates to enforce the compulsory muzzling of dogs. This was rather ineffective, owing to the reluctance of dog owners to comply with it. Thus twenty years later, in 1897, Parliament gave the police power to seize stray dogs and at the same time imposed a quarantine period of six months for imported dogs. These stringent measures succeeded and rabies disappeared from Britain in 1903. These successful steps were directed only towards domestic stock and it is again evident that rabies in Britain did not then appear to be endemic in wildlife. This is in notable contrast to many other regions.

Of the various possible chains involved in the transfer of rabies between wild animals and humans or their stock in different parts of the world, that in the Arctic appears to be one of the more straightforward. For centuries Eskimos have described a form of canine madness which more recently became known as Arctic dog disease and was diagnosed by Plummer as rabies in 1947. Kantorovich (1957) showed that there were some serological differences in polar disease from normal rabies (he found 73 strains) probably due to slight changes in the virus in this extreme habitat (see also Konavalov, Kantorovich, Buzinov, and Riutova 1965). An outbreak of Arctic dog disease (or polar madness) reached a peak among wolves and foxes in the 1940s and thereafter continued for a decade (Williams 1969). Biologists often turn to polar regions in attempts to understand aspects of ecology because of the simplicity of the polar ecosystems: a simplicity, it should be stressed, which is only relative. Both North American and Russian workers who have studied Arctic rabies agree that the reservoir of the disease is the Arctic fox, *Alopex lagopus* (Crandell 1975). Rausch (1958) believes that the occurrence of the disease in wolves and coyotes represents the occasional overspill from the Arctic-fox population. Interestingly, he suggests that the low occurrence of rabies among Eskimos is a result of their thick clothing. One of the diseases that may mimic rabies is canine hepatitis, and it may be that the dogs were actually ill with that disease. Similarly, canine distemper may mimic rabies, and even among rabid dogs only 75 per cent have virus in the salivary glands and only 60 per cent have enough to infect man.

Iceland, now quite free of rabies, has also suffered outbreaks in the past. In 1731 a strange 'plague' in dogs spread to foxes in the Snaefellsnes peninsula: 'foxes approached farms where they behaved strangely towards dogs and other domestic animals, and even staggered into fishermen's huts and other dwellings and walked, crazed, into people's hands' (Helgason 1960).† Later in 1766 in Nordfjordur another outbreak led to the following account: 'some say the reason is that an English skipper, who thought that Arni, farmer in Nes, had cheated him in trade over spirits, had put a spell on a bitch at the farm. The bitch became mad and bit its own pup and both died before long. This madness spread to other dogs . . .' (Helgason 1961).†

A major outbreak of Arctic rabies occurred in the 1960s in Greenland, during which more than 1000 dogs died. Steele (1973) has reviewed this epizooty. In addition to the canine suffering involved, these losses constituted a serious economic problem for Greenland.

One particularly important fact to emerge from studies of Arctic fox rabies comes from the work of the Russian scientist Kantorovich, who with his colleagues reported in 1963 that he had found rabies virus in the nervous systems of apparently healthy Arctic foxes. This suggested the possibility that some animals may act as carriers for the virus without succumbing to it. In later studies, however, Kantorovich stated that the explanation was that the foxes had been killed at the end of the incubation period.

While a low incidence of human death is a feature of Arctic rabies, this was not so in Europe in the past. For instance, in France between 1851 and 1877, there were 770 human deaths from rabies. Of these, 707 followed bites from rabid dogs, 38 from wolves, 23 from cats, and one each from fox and cow. Of all people dying from rabies during the late nineteenth century in Europe, about 90 per cent were infected by dogs

† Both passages translated by P. Hersteinsson.

and 4 per cent by cats. Of wildlife species, wolves accounted for a further 4 per cent and foxes for only 2 per cent. During the present European outbreak dogs again pose a considerable threat to their owners; in West Berlin 221 people were given anti-rabies post-exposure (prophylactic) treatment in 1975. These people had all been bitten by animals that were potentially rabid, and of these 149 (67.4 per cent) were dogs and 32 (14.5 per cent) were cats. Only eight bites were from foxes (3.6 per cent). The statistics for the animal victims of the disease are very different. For instance, the French authorities have kept detailed figures on the number of animals reported with rabies in France. Taking as an example cases reported between March 1968 and December 1975, the total was 9465, of which 78.5 per cent were foxes and 10.2 per cent cattle. Similar figures from West Germany show that of 50 617 animal cases reported between 1954 and 1972 63.5 per cent were foxes.

For the most part, the enormous reduction in the number of dogs infected with rabies nowadays is a consequence of compulsory dog vaccination and control of strays. Corey and Hattwick (1975) have shown that dog vaccination was associated with a fall in the number of cases of canine rabies in America: from 5000 in 1946 to 180 in 1973. But while the number of cases of rabid dogs in the United States fell by 96 per cent between 1953 and 1971, the number of infected cats decreased by only 59 per cent during the same period.

In Europe also cats continue to be a problem. Of 79 rabid domestic animals reported in Switzerland between 1967 and 1970, 40 were cats while only six were dogs; and it was cats that caused three out of 23 deaths from rabies among people in East Germany between 1953 and 1961, and also caused 15 out of the 25 deaths in Hungary during the same period.

Although the British have been alerted to the potential dangers from fox-borne rabies should it reach their shores, it is noteworthy that the direct risk to people is mainly from dogs. The problem once rabies gets into a fox population is not direct risk to people, but the difficulty of eliminating this reservoir of infection. In countries where vaccination of domestic stock has disrupted the bridge between wildlife rabies and human beings and where there is also good post-exposure treatment for people who are bitten, the risk appears to be rather small. Of six human deaths in America between 1970 and 1973, none in fact resulted from fox bites; while of the 56 human cases in America between 1950 and 1970 only six were caused by foxes, 21 being caused by dogs or cats, ten by skunks, and seven by bats. In France there have been no deaths from rabies since 1946. The main reasons for the low incidence of human rabies within the rabies epizootic area are massive pre- and post-exposure prophylaxis and dog immunization. In general, then, the risk of dying from rabies in affluent societies is slightly less than that of being struck by lightning. It is for this reason that many onlookers view the British preoccupation with rabies with certain puzzlement. Nevertheless, to judge the problem trivial would be wrong; the toll of human deaths from rabies in affluent societies may be small, but the presence of rabies does seriously disrupt public peace of mind. It could be argued that this would be particularly so in Britain, where the current very relaxed attitude towards wildlife permits desirable changes in the approach to conservation. Furthermore there are good reasons to believe that were rabies endemic in the British Isles, it could pose a more serious hazard than in many other European countries; on these small islands are crowded 55 million people together with 6 million domestic dogs and a further 6 million domestic cats. Added to this, many towns in Britain now have a sizeable urban fox population which probably has nightly contact with domestic animals—a dangerous recipe for the transmission of urban rabies into wildlife. Of course, there are many improbable bridges to be crossed by the rabies virus before it becomes established in British wildlife, and the risks may be very slight indeed. Nevertheless it is prudent to consider these risks and to prepare contingency plans.

There is a second reason, global rather than local, for considering the rabies problem more seriously than might have seemed necessary on the basis of the death toll reported for Europe and America. These are affluent societies, where large sums have already been spent in prophylaxis and other control measures. In many parts of the developing world rabies poses a much greater threat to human life, and throughout much of the tropics it causes enormous financial losses to farmers. Most of the countries in which rabies is a prevalent disease have no accurate statistics on its incidence, but it has been suggested that there are 15 000 deaths in the world each year caused by rabies; some authorities estimate 10 000 deaths for India alone. The extent of the threat to some communities is illustrated by Warrell's (1977) account for the Philippines (date from Arambulo and Escudero 1971):

The Philippines has a population of about 32 million human beings and 3.7 million dogs. In 1964, 383 human beings and about 25 000 dogs died of rabies, an incidence in man of 1.2 per hundred thousand population. These deaths occurred despite the vaccination of 150 000 people each year (½ per cent of the population) following dog bites.

So far as is known, Sri Lanka has the highest incidence of rabies with 140 human deaths per annum out of a population of 11.5 million.

In 1966, FAO surveyed the incidence of rabies in cattle in Latin America between Mexico and northern Argentina, where the disease was introduced in 1806 by the sporting dogs of English officers. In that area they estimated that one million cattle die annually of rabies transmitted by vampire bats. The discovery that these bats were one of the agents transmitting rabies to cattle goes back to 1908 when a bovine disease (*mal de caderas*) was rampant in southern Brazil. Ranchers noticed that vampire bats were flying during the day and fighting with one another and indeed biting cattle. In 1916 rabies virus was isolated from a bat caught in the act of biting a cow. The direct economic loss in Latin America through rabies exceeds US $250 million annually, and indirect losses such as those through malnutrition, exacerbated by loss of livestock, may cost another 250 thousand million dollars annually (Acha 1966). In Latin America 250 000 people are treated for possible exposure to rabies annually (Acha and Fernandes 1976). In the Arctic the epidemiology of rabies may be relatively simple and associated primarily with one species, the Arctic fox, but in both South and North America the situation is greatly complicated by the presence of a variety of potential vectors. In South America these are mostly vampire and other bats but also include various species of canid animals and other carnivores. In North America both red and grey foxes are implicated, together with two species of skunks and racoons and, in Mexico, coatis. In South Africa and Rhodesia various species of mongoose may also act as a reservoir for the disease (Tierkel 1959). Mongooses were introduced to most of the larger Caribbean Islands between 1870 and 1900 but mongoose-transmitted rabies is found only on Cuba, Hispaniola, Puerto Rico, and Grenada. All the other Caribbean Islands are free of rabies except Trinidad, where it is transmitted by bats.

In summary, rabies presents problems of different sorts in different parts of the world. In the developing world it not only constitutes a serious risk to human life, but may also exert considerable influence on national economies through losses to livestock. Among more affluent societies the risk to people can be regarded as minimal, albeit at considerable cost. Nevertheless, present-day attempts to minimize this risk entail serious impact on wildlife species, in particular the red fox. In addition, while human life itself may be at small risk, rabies threatens our peace of mind and may disenchant our feelings for the countryside. It is clearly not only desirable to keep Britain free of the disease, but also where it is endemic to find some solution which will reduce its incidence in wildlife.

In Chapter 3 I shall discuss the epidemiology of the disease in some European countries in more detail and the attempts that have been made to control its spread in fox populations. First, however, I shall give more detailed description of the disease, its clinical symptoms, and the mechanism of infection.

2 Medical aspects of rabies

The disease rabies is caused by a bullet-shaped virus measuring only 140 × 100 nanometres (a nanometre is one-millionth of a millimetre); about 40 would stretch across a red blood corpuscle. Research has shown that the core of the rabies virus consists of two components, an internal helical structure of nucleic acid surrounded by a layer of protein. This core is in turn surrounded by a membranous envelope which is covered by small spikes. These spikes consist chemically of a glycoprotein and are thought to be important in the attachment of the virus to susceptible cells. When a virus enters a susceptible cell its nucleic acid is exposed, becomes active and takes over the cellular mechanisms, using them to synthesize virus nucleic acid, proteins, and other substances, instead of new cellular material. The various components are assembled into new virus particles which are able to infect uninfected cells of the host organism. The presence of virus multiplying in host cells is responsible for the symptoms of the disease.

The proteins which envelop the virus nucleic acid are antigenic: they may stimulate the host animal to produce a special type of protein, known as antibody, which can interact specifically with the stimulating antigen. Antibodies to some virus protein have the power to neutralize the infectivity of the virus. Antibodies which neutralize rabies virus are active against the glycoprotein of the virus's coat.

Most viruses enter the body by being inhaled (e.g. psittacosis), or through a scratch (cat-scratch disease), or through the bite of an insect (yellow fever). Having entered they attack susceptible cells and the incubation period of the disease begins. Most diseases have fairly well defined incubation periods between infection and the onset of symptoms. In rabies the incubation period is variable. This is partly due to the mechanism whereby the infecting virus reaches its target cells. (See the discussion by Gordon Smith (1964) of virus transmission.)

The rabies virus travels to the brain via the peripheral nerves. Thus when rabies virus is present in the saliva of an infected animal which then bites a victim, the virus is injected into the victim's muscle. (This was first demonstrated by Zinke in 1804.) After some local multiplication of variable extent, the virus enters the peripheral nerves. Nerve fibres are made up of a central axon along which impulses travel and the axon is surrounded by a membrane (the myelin sheath). The rabies virus makes its way into the axon cylinder and thereafter migrates through the system towards the spinal cord and ultimately to the brain. Once in the brain the virus multiplies and then moves out along the nerves again to the peripheral organs. Since nerves lead to almost every part of the body they serve as routes which ensure that the rabies virus ultimately reaches almost every tissue of its victim's body. In particular the virus rapidly reaches the salivary glands and hence when this animal in turn bites another victim the cycle can begin again. L. Andral (personal communication) has found that 1 ml of the contents of a rabid fox's salivary gland diluted 34 millionfold can still result in infection; theoretically, with two salivary glands, each fox might infect 67.5 million others, but in practice, to keep an enzootic extant, rabid foxes bite one or two other foxes.

The frenzied rage which typifies the minority of rabies cases and provokes the rabid animal to bite apparently indiscriminately is a consequence of the virus multiplying in the cells of the brain. These rabies-induced frenzies typify the popular image of an infected animal but furious rabies is not the only manifestation of the disease. Another form is dumb rabies in which the animal suffers from a creeping paralysis. Animals suffering from these less spectacular symptoms are none the less dangerous since they may pass the disease on simply by licking, if their saliva comes into contact with a small cut or abrasion. Over 50 per cent of infected foxes exhibit dumb symptoms. It is unknown why it is advantageous to the virus to have these proportions of dumb and furious symptoms. Presumbly they have evolved in response to aspects of the hosts' behaviour in disease transmission.

For all practical purposes the route whereby rabies virus infects man is through a break in the skin. However, it is conceivable that the virus could enter the body through an intact mucous membrane such as that covering the eye or lining the mouth and lung. In this way laboratory animals can be infected by eating contaminated food. Furthermore, a 14-year-old girl from Georgia died of rabies (in spite of Pasteur treatment) in 1939 having on several occasions permitted a rabid dog to lick her genitalia (Leach and Johnson 1940). Even more unfair is the case of the Idaho woman who, in 1978, died having received a corneal transplant from a man who had been incubating rabies.†

In the 1950s two men died of rabies after exploring caves in Texas. The caves were inhabited by Mexican freetailed bats, *Tadarida braziliensis*. Some were found to be infected with rabies and the air in the cave supported a fine suspension of the virus emanating from the bats' saliva and urine. The men may have inhaled the rabies virus or perhaps it entered from the air through abrasions in their skin. Similarly a veterinary surgeon who died in 1972 after working with rabid goat brain which he had been emulsifying probably inhaled the virus in aerosol form. The ancient Greeks feared infection from standing in urine from

† *New England Journal of Medicine* **300**, 608.

mad dogs. Any abrasions on the feet were then treated with warm horse manure sprinkled with vinegar! In countries where dogs may be rabid the risk from their bites is serious: Warrell (1977) quotes horrifying figures for the number of dog bites handled routinely by hospitals every year. For example, in America 0.5 per cent of the population is bitten each year, while up to 15 per cent of children aged between 2 and 10 years are bitten. He quotes figures from one part of Liverpool where 1 person in 200 is bitten by a dog every year and in Sunderland where 1 in 250 children of under 15 years of age is bitten each year. The enormous task that would be involved if each of these dog-bite victims had to be screened for rabies in those two towns alone gives some inkling of the strain the presence of rabies in Britain could put on the National Health Service.

One of the most distressing features of rabies for potential victims is the unpredictability of the interval between the bite which introduces the virus into the body and the ultimate appearance of symptoms of the disease. The incubation period is so variable that the victim may wait months still fearing he may have the disease. About 85 per cent of cases have an incubation period of between 2 and 8 weeks, part of the variation being explained by the distance from the wound to the central nervous system. Once the incubation period is over the patient starts to show symptoms of the disease. The fact that these are extremely variable frequently precludes rapid diagnosis; most of the symptoms are not unique to rabies (e.g. nausea, stomach-aches, and diarrhoea), nor indeed shared universally by all rabies victims. Warrell reports that one early symptom apparently shared by most patients is a tingling numbness or ache emanating from around the site of the original bite, even if that has long since healed. Thereafter if the brain is seriously affected the patient may develop furious rabies; alternatively if the spinal cord is involved predominantly, paralytic or dumb rabies will ensue. Perhaps the best-known human symptom of the disease is hydrophobia—fear of water. At the sight of water the patient suffers spasms of the diaphragm and other respiratory muscles, sometimes so severe that the whole body arches backwards. This is accompanied by terror. The patient may retch so violently as to rip the junction between the oesophagus and the stomach. His cries are distorted through inflammation of the vocal cords so that his voice sounds more like a dog's bark. Even a draught of cool air blowing in a patient's face may trigger this horrifying response.

Most patients with paralytic rabies do not suffer hydrophobia. The best-known outbreak of paralytic rabies occurred between 1929 and 1931 in Trinidad when 20 people died. For the most part these patients were unaware of being bitten by anything although one woman reported having seen a bat fly from the end of her bed during the night whereupon she had discovered that her toe was bleeding. Initially this outbreak was thought to be a form of poliomyelitis or perhaps of food poisoning, but finally rabies virus was isolated.

Potentially a rabid human being could infect other people but this has never been documented. Nevertheless, one reads heroic accounts of victims demanding, in moments of lucidity, to be chained down lest they infect those around them. The mother of the seventeenth-century microscopist, Marcello Malpighi was reputedly bitten by her own daughter and subsequently both mother and daughter died from rabies.

Can rabies be cured? Once a patient has been bitten by an animal with rabies and so infected he may be treated with post-exposure vaccine. At this stage (*before* symptoms develop) the progress of the disease may be halted. Baer and Cleary (1972) have indicated that rabies virus injected into mice may remain at the peripheral inoculation site for as long as 18 days. Murphy and Bauer (1974) obtained similar results working on hamsters, and suggest that the initial infection of muscle may be an amplifying phase during which sufficient virus is built up to invade the peripheral nervous system. It may be during this period that post-exposure vaccination is effective. Various sorts of vaccines will be discussed later (p. 115).

If treatment is attempted *after* symptoms have manifested, complete cure is rarely, if ever, achieved. The technique used after symptoms appear employs artificial life-support systems such as mechanical ventilation of the lungs and artificial regulation of heartbeats by a cardiac pacemaker. These support systems may prolong the life of a patient with rabies, sometimes for over 100 days. The hope is that if life can be prolonged enough, then the patient may survive (see discussion by Warrell *et al.* 1976). This intensive-care treatment may have two successes to its credit: the American child, Matthew Winkler, who was bitten by a rabid bat when aged six and a middle-aged Argentinian woman who was bitten in the arm by a dog. Intensive care resulted in the survival of both patients but the woman took over a year to achieve a complete recovery. However, there is a debate among doctors as to whether either case constitutes a genuine cure of a natural infection.

While a human patient who develops symptoms of rabies faces the prospect of almost certain death, this is not necessarily the outcome for other species. Various bats and some carnivores (including a dog in Ethiopia reported by Andral) seem either to recover from the infection or carry the virus in a latent form for variable periods. In fact, although the rabies virus was previously considered to be a single serological entity, it is now known to have affinities with four other viruses, including the Mokola virus which affects man (Shope and Tignor 1971).

3 The epizootiology of vulpine rabies: a detailed examination

Rabies has occurred periodically in waves throughout history; Europe is currently undergoing such a wave. In this chapter I shall examine in detail the progress of rabies during an epizootic, concentrating in particular on the involvement of the red fox.

The present European rabies epizootic began south of Gdansk in Poland in 1939, since when it has spread over 1000 miles across north-west Europe. The disease reached the Elbe in 1950 and the Rhine in 1960, and entered France in 1968 when 63 cases of animal rabies were confirmed. This progression is schematized in Fig. 3.1. A better idea of the magnitude of the problem in Europe is given in Table 3.1 which summarizes the number of cases in each of seven European countries between 1965 and 1972 as the disease spread. In 1965 rabies was already well entrenched in West Germany, 3910 cases being reported. This table lumps together all reported cases but the majority were foxes, cattle, or domestic dogs and cats. The figures for both Luxembourg and Belgium are interesting: the data show that having been invaded in 1966, both countries were almost free of rabies again at the end of 1970. In contrast after the infection entered France in 1968, the number of cases continued to increase until 1972. The spread of the disease west-wards involved the successive infection of Denmark in 1964, Belgium, Luxembourg, and Austria in 1966, Switzerland in 1967, France in 1968, and Holland in 1974. Similarly, the disease spread through Poland southwards to Czechoslovakia and Hungary.

Table 3.1   Cases of rabies observed between 1965 and 1972 in West Germany and countries subsequently infected

Country	1965	1966	1967	1968	1969	1970	1971	1972
West Germany	3910	3661	4373	4353	3917	2036	2214	2524
Denmark	52	1	0	1	71	83	0	0
Austria	0	8	79	173	93	116	213	78
Belgium	0	40	326	453	161	20	4	7
Luxembourg	0	49	294	31	12	11	0	0
Switzerland	0	0	193	713	393	295	353	499
France	0	0	0	63	334	513	896	1027

Data from the Centre National d'Études sur la Rage.

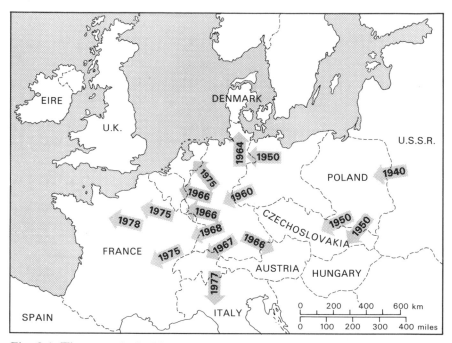

Fig. 3.1. The spread of rabies in Europe, 1940–1979.

As successive European governments react to the invasion by rabies with vaccination and 'watchdog' campaigns, the proportion of cases involving domestic stock and pets is reduced and the proportion involving foxes increases. This is illustrated by figures collected in Poland by Mol (1971), who showed that in 1966, 29.3 per cent rabies infections diagnosed were in foxes, while by 1971, 70.6 per cent were in foxes. This was because the number of cases due to foxes remained constant, but the proportion increased since involvement of domestic pets was eliminated. In a relatively small area such as Belgium or Luxembourg the incidence of the disease typically shows a rhythmic fluctuation with a period of from 3 to 7 years separating successive peaks or troughs. This is demonstrated in Table 3.1 and Fig. 3.2 which show the annual incidence of rabies in Belgium and Luxembourg between its entry in 1966 and 1977 when, especially in Belgium, a second wave had passed through the countries. In order to give a clearer impression of rabies epizootiology I shall consider in more detail certain examples, beginning with France.

France

Since it was first recorded in France in 1968 the number of rabies cases has increased steadily from year to year. By 1970, six departments

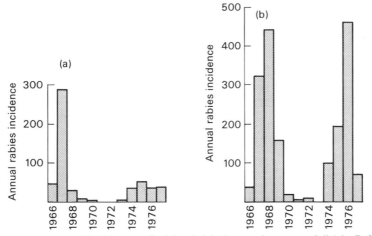

Fig. 3.2. The annual incidence of rabies (a) in Luxembourg and (b) in Belgium from 1966 to 1977. (Data from the Centre National d'Études sur la Rage.)

were infected (Moselle, Ardennes, Meuse, Meurthe-et-Moselle, Bas-Rhin, and Marne). Figure 3.3 shows the progress of the epizootic front in France over the years. The annual number of cases increased quite dramatically from 63 during 1968 to 1027 in 1972 to nearly 3000 in 1976. Figure 3.4 shows the increase year by year in the number of cases of rabies. In 1976 the total of 2918 cases comprised 62 dogs, 111 cats, 273 cattle, and 2279 foxes. In 1978, 1200 cases comprised 40 dogs, 46 cats, 931 foxes, and less than 200 cattle. Of course these figures given here are subject to very serious sampling bias in that the large majority of domestic stock contracting the disease will be examined by scientists whereas only a proportion of wild foxes succumbing will be discovered. For this reason Andral (personal communication) estimates that the number of foxes reported with rabies is an underestimate of between one-half and one-fifth of the total number dying (see Braunschweig 1980).

The annual totals of cases in France include many varieties of different species, and there has been a general increase in most of them with successive years. Thus for instance, of the 2029 cases in 1975, 38 were in dogs, 74 in cats, 91 in cattle, and 1719 in foxes; in each species there has been an increase in the incidence of the disease between 1975 and 1976. Interestingly, after a peak in 1971 there had, until 1976, been a steady decline in the number of cases of bovine rabies reported in France from year to year, in spite of the steady increase in the area engulfed by the epizooty. Fluctuations in the incidence of bovine rabies have been considered by Andral and Toma (1977). They argue that the dramatic fall in the incidence of bovine rabies in 1971 followed the introduction of

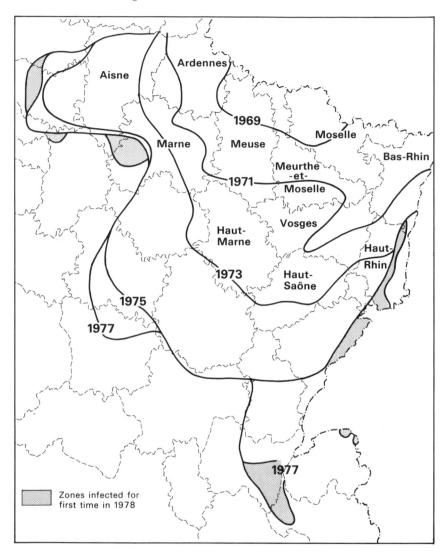

Fig. 3.3. The advance of rabies in France. The lines show the position of the epizootic front at 2-year intervals. Further details for the named departments are given in Table 3.2. (Data from the Centre National d'Études sur la Rage.)

a large vaccination scheme to protect the cattle. The sudden resurgence of the disease in 1976 principally involved only four departments: in Meuse there were 100 cases, in Meurthe-et-Moselle there were 72, while in Ardennes there were 35, and in Moselle 20. Indeed, Andral and Toma report that 83 per cent of the 273 cases of bovine tuberculosis

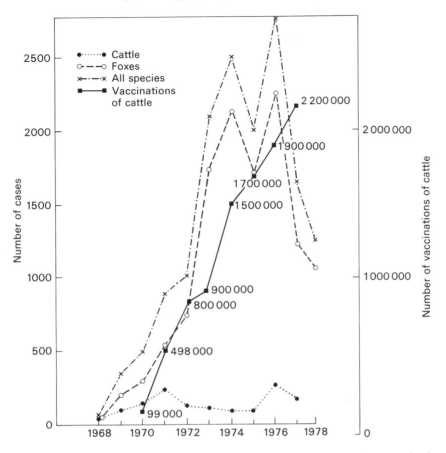

Fig. 3.4. The incidence of cases of rabies in foxes, cattle, and other species in France from 1968 to 1978. These figures are plotted together with the number of cattle vaccinated each year against rabies. The graph shows an inverse relationship between the number of cases of bovine rabies and the number of vaccinations. Since 1975 vaccination has been gradually superseded by farmers taking out insurance policies against rabies. This cheaper alternative is considered to be a mistake in the long term by the Centre National d'Études sur la Rage. (Data from the Centre National d'Études sur la Rage.)

reported in France in 1976 were in these four departments. This contrasts dramatically with the situation for fox rabies in the same area where only 24.4 per cent of the 2279 cases were confined to these same departments. These figures provoke some confusion in the light of the conventional situation where rabies in foxes and other species increased together. The figures are made more striking when one considers that in these four eastern departments of France, only 2.45 rabid foxes were found for each rabid cow in contrast to the remainder of France where 37.4 rabid foxes were found for each rabid cow.

The explanation of the figures appears to lie in a false sense of security

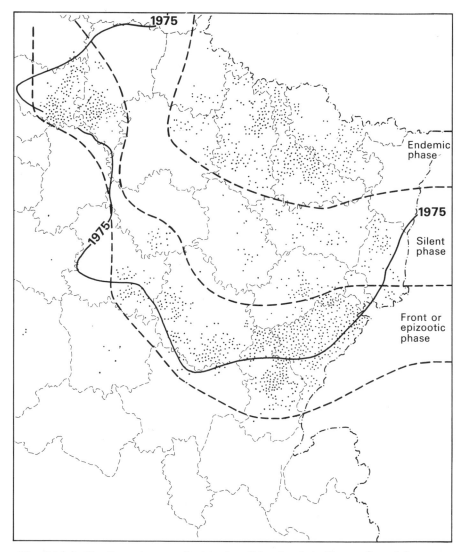

Fig. 3.5(a). Confirmed cases of rabies in wild animals in France from 1 January to 31 December 1976 showing broad divisions into different phases of the epizootic. (Data from the Centre National d'Études sur la Rage.)

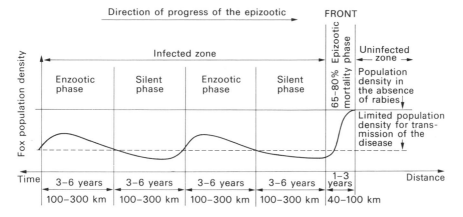

Fig. 3.5(b). Fluctuations in fox population density as a function of the passage of a rabies epizootic. (Data from the Centre National d'Études sur la Rage.)

engendered by the apparent passing of the epizooty. The four departments in question can be seen, from the map (Fig. 3.3), to be among those first infected with the disease. Consequently, they are now a considerable distance from the front of the epizootic and in less frequent contact with ailing foxes or other signs of the disease. This appears to have induced a certain lethargy among farmers towards the vaccination campaign and, indeed, in the year 1975–6 only 6 per cent of the cattle in the four departments were vaccinated in contrast to 80 per cent which were vaccinated in departments near to the front of the epizooty. In fact, insurance against rabies in cattle is cheaper than inoculation with vaccine.

Although the incidence of bovine rabies may be closely related to the enthusiasm with which farmers pursue vaccination schedules, 1976 did witness an interesting natural feature of rabies epizootiology in France. The Centre National d'Études sur la Rage records the location of every reported case of animal rabies throughout the year and these are pictured for 1976 in Fig. 3.5(a). This shows clearly that there were three areas where the disease was particularly rampant, one to the west around Oise, a second more to the south in Jura, and a third within those departments first occupied by the disease in 1968, particularly the Ardennes, Meuse, Meurthe-et-Moselle, Moselle, and Bas-Rhin. The foremost two centres of the epizooty represent part of the continuing advance of the front but the third centre in those departments originally infected was a new phenomenon in 1976. This is clear from data for the preceding year, 1975, when there was also a westward centre and a southerly one but only a low incidence of infection near the German border. This resurgence of the disease in an area which it had passed through some years beforehand is interpreted by Andral as the first evidence from France of a succession of waves of infection sweeping through the fox population as schematized in Fig. 3.5(b) (see also Andral and Toma 1977). The history of rabies in one of the departments that is suffering a resurgence of the disease is pictured in the histogram in Fig. 3.6, where the pattern can be seen for Ardennes. The absolute numbers of cases of rabies in different departments are very different. Some of this difference may be explained by variation in the extent of good fox habitat, but the intensity of hunting or searching effort for foxes and other factors determining fox density may be pertinent. These will be considered in the next chapter.

So far I have mentioned foxes and cattle as the two main victims of rabies in France, but other species are involved on a lesser scale. In the laboratory, scientists have demonstrated that almost every species of mammal can be infected with rabies; but susceptibility varies enormously between species; in the field the incidence of rabies in different species varies similarly. For example, the susceptibility of foxes is extremely high, as is that of other canids such as coyotes, jackals, and

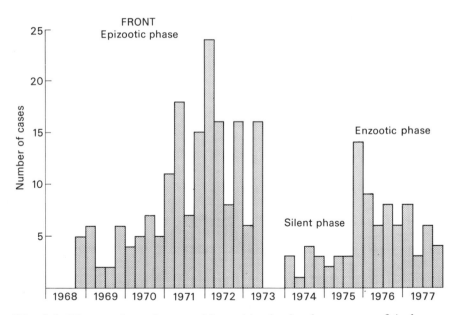

Fig. 3.6. The number of cases of fox rabies in the department of Ardennes recorded each quarter from late 1968 to 1977 (Data from the Centre National d'Études sur la Rage.)

wolves, and some rodents such as field voles. In contrast animals like skunks, racoons, domestic cats, cattle, and rodents are only moderately susceptible although perhaps more so than sheep, goats, and horses. These differences in susceptibility to the disease are perhaps reflected in figures taken between 1968 and 1973 for the incidence of rabies amongst different species in various departments in France. These figures are presented in Table 3.2 and while they clearly show enormous numbers of rabid foxes compared to other species, for example badgers, they do present some difficulties of interpretation because of biases in the accuracy with which each species is sampled. For example, in the category 'other species' are a number of small carnivores such as weasels, stoats, or polecats and it is almost certain that the incidence of rabies in these species, which are seldom seen by man, is likely to be grossly underestimated. One interesting feature of Table 3.2 is the decline in numbers of dogs and cats contracting the disease. Just as with agricultural stock, compulsory vaccination schemes have drastically

Table 3.2　The number of cases of rabies certified in the east of France for the period 26 March 1968 to 31 May 1973

| Department | Wild animals | | | | Domestic animals | | | | | | Total for all species |
| | | | | | Carnivores | | Herbivores and pigs | | | | |
	Foxes	Badgers	Roe	Other species	Dogs	Cats	Cattle	Sheep goats	Horses	Pigs	
Aisne	5	—	—	—	—	1	1	—	—	—	7
Ardennes	176	2	—	3	15	16	138	3	2	1	356
Marne	120	1	1	3	4	8	15	3	—	—	155
Haute-Marne	156	1	—	4	3	1	7	1	—	—	173
Meurthe-et-Moselle	463	6	3	3	19	17	156	11	9	—	687
Meuse	504	2	8	18	24	35	257	30	9	2	889
Moselle	178	2	6	3	18	21	104	5	2	—	339
Bas-Rhin	323	8	15	4	10	12	11	3	1	—	387
Haut-Rhin	16	1	1	—	—	—	—	—	—	—	18
Haute-Saône	123	4	—	—	—	1	2	5	1	—	136
Vosges	658	32	—	6	12	15	6	5	—	—	734
Total	2722	59	34	44	105	127	697	66	24	3	3881
Percentages	70		3.5		2.7	3.3	18		2.4		100

Data from the Centre National d'Études sur la Rage.

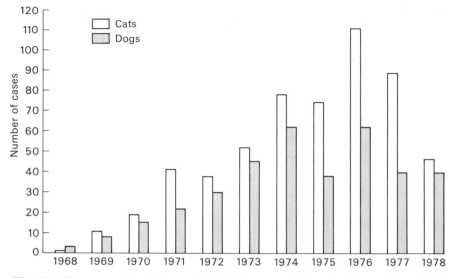

Fig. 3.7. The annual incidence of rabies in cats and dogs in France from 1968 to 1978. (Data from the Centre National d'Études sur la Rage.)

reduced the numbers of these domestic pets succumbing to the disease and hence minimized the risk to their owners. It is worth noticing that the cases of cat rabies outnumber those of dogs (cats are less frequently vaccinated than dogs). This is shown in more detail in Fig. 3.7 for the years 1968 to 1978. The possibility of transmission between cats and foxes, particularly in the British Isles between cats and urban foxes, is one that deserves serious consideration; for example Andral (personal communication) has found 9.8 per cent of feral cats to be rabid from a sample of 61 (in contrast to 3.8 per cent of house cats).

For recent European rabies the pre-eminence of the fox amongst identified cases in general, as illustrated by Kauker's (1975) data shown in Table 3.3. These data show that for 11 European countries the minimum incidence of *recorded* fox rabies compared to other wild animals and domestic stock is 68 per cent (in Belgium), while Hungary presents the other extreme with 85 per cent of identified rabies cases among foxes.

The idea that parasites might be involved in the chain of rabies transmission, for instance between foxes, has been explored by Aubert and Andral (1975). They found rabies virus in certain ticks parasitic upon mammals. Hence one cannot discount the possibility that ecto-parasites may influence rabies epizootiology, especially in areas temporarily free of rabies after the passage of the disease front.

Table 3.3 Percentage of rabies cases identified
in various groups of animal species in
European countries

Country	Foxes	Other wild animals	Domestic animals
West Germany	69.0	11.5	18.5
East Germany	75.3	8.5	16.2
Austria	79.0	16.0	5.0
Belgium	68.0	4.2	27.8
Luxembourg	69.4	9.0	21.6
Switzerland	80.6	12.9	6.5
France	75.4	3.8	20.8
Denmark	79.3	5.2	15.5
Poland	70.6	4.4	25.0
Hungary	85.0	2.0	13.0
Czechoslovakia	77.0	5.2	17.8

Source: Kauker (1975).

Similarly, rodents may be implicated too: Botros *et al.* (1976) working in Egypt, examined 549 rodents (13 species) and 95 other wild mammals (7 species). They isolated rabies virus from the brains of 3 out of 273 gerbils (1.1 per cent) and 1 out of 56 foxes (1.8 per cent). They cautiously concluded that it would be unwise not to recommend anti-rabies treatment for rodent bites in Egypt.

At the Centre National d'Études sur la Rage monthly records are kept of each rabies case reported in France. This project, together with similar ones in other European countries, allows comparison between the incidence of vulpine rabies at different times of the year. Such studies reveal a consistent drop in the number of cases reported each year during the late spring and early summer with a peak during March. This trend is shown in Fig. 3.8 which presents a monthly incidence of fox rabies between June 1968 and June 1969 in West Germany. There is also a seasonal cycle in the monthly occurrence of rabies in cattle, and this is shown by Toma and Andral's (1977) data in Fig. 3.9. Clearly there is not only a peak in bovine rabies each year, but this peak occurs earlier than that in the fox population, namely in November and December. The seasonal fluctuations in the incidence of bovine rabies are apparently tied to agricultural practice; the cattle are confined to byres during certain months and during this period the probability of exposure to rabies from wildlife is greatly reduced. In fact because of the interval between exposure to the disease and development of the

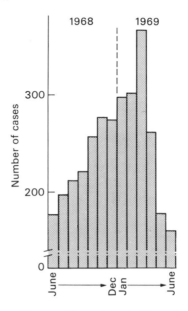

Fig. 3.8. The monthly incidence of fox rabies in West Germany from June 1968 to June 1969. (From Toma and Andral 1977.)

symptoms the peak incidence of rabies occurs while the cattle are inside farm buildings. While this explanation suffices for seasonal variation in bovine rabies, it raises the question of what could explain the pattern observed among the fox population. This question will be considered in the next chapter.

The Netherlands

Rabies reached the Netherlands much more recently than it did France, the first case of vulpine infection being reported in 1974. A survey of rabies epidemiology conducted by Niewold and his colleagues in Holland in 1977 serves to demonstrate that the disease there is following a pattern similar to that in other European countries.

The Dutch were alerted to the impending danger in 1962 when there was an outbreak of the disease among domestic stock in Amsterdam, although there was still no immediate threat from wildlife rabies. This outbreak, presumed to be the consequence of the illegal importation of a domestic dog, resulted in the death of five people and eight animals. It also prompted the enactment of the Cattle Act authorizing the detention and destruction of livestock on the basis of suspected rabies infection. Similarly, the vaccination of dogs and cats and the leashing and muzzling

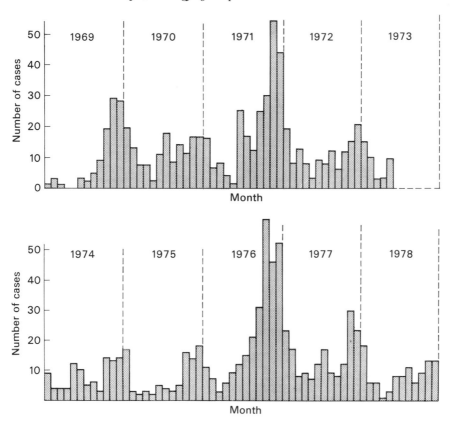

Fig. 3.9. The monthly incidence of bovine rabies in France from 1969 to 1978. (From Toma and Andral 1977.)

of dogs became statutory at the same time. Other measures included the destruction of stray dogs and feral cats together with the prohibition of such events as dog shows. It was not until 1967 that wildlife rabies began to approach the Zuid-Limburg area of Holland from both the Belgian and German frontiers. In response, the Dutch authorities revitalized the campaign for compulsory vaccination of dogs and the destruction of strays and also of wild foxes was intensified. In fact rabies was not recorded in Holland until 1974 and since then there have been approximately 50 cases.

These have been concentrated in three areas, initially in the north around Oost-Groningen, then in 1975 in Oost-Overijssel, and lastly in 1976 in the area that seemed to be threatened originally, Zuid-Limburg.

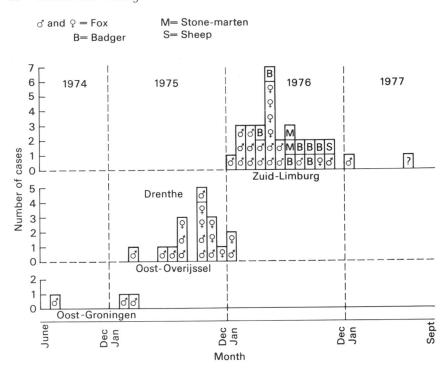

Fig. 3.10. Outbreaks of rabies in Zuid-Limburg, Oost-Overijssel, and Oost-Groningen recorded by month, species, and sex of fox during 1974–7. (Data from F. Niewold.)

Most cases have involved foxes but there have been seven positive diagnoses among badgers, two among stone-martens, and one of a sheep. The monthly occurrence of diagnosed rabies in each of these areas is presented, by species, in Fig. 3.10 which also includes information on the sex of the foxes involved. Although the sample sizes are small, it does seem that in each case male foxes are implicated first and only thereafter are vixens infected.

Poland

The present rabies epizootic has been entrenched in Poland since the 1940s but has undergone some interesting changes, as documented by Mol (1977). During the early post-war years rabies was spread through dogs in Poland, but in 1948 compulsory canine vaccination was introduced, and by 1956 the toll had fallen to a fiftieth of its previous level.

During the years up until 1956 wildlife rabies was rare (1–7 cases per annum), but from then on rabies became common in wild species, particularly foxes which comprised 72.5 per cent of the 1622 confirmed cases in 1975. Mol reviews these changes in the context of a methodical poisoning campaign against birds of prey and against crows which began in 1954. This has resulted in the extermination of some species and reduced the previously abundant crow to a rarity. Mol believes that an indirect consequence of the reduction in numbers of these birds has resulted in a greater abundance of rodents and hence higher fox populations and so the increase of rabies in wildlife. Indeed, he pinpoints provinces within Poland where rodent numbers are known to be particularly high and prone to cyclical peaks and shows that these are the same provinces in which fox rabies most frequently occurs.

Rabies is a more stringent method of fox control than any yet devised by man. The Polish authorities believe that none of the available methods are effective and so they rely instead on rabies. Thus by an order signed in 1962 they draw an 'infected circle' around an outbreak, in which stray dogs and cats are killed and ailing foxes destroyed, but where the disease is then left to run its course. It is assumed that the outbreak will reduce the number of foxes more effectively than any human interference and without the associated disturbance. Mol (1977) stresses that the most effective procedure to fight rabies would be the protection of all birds of prey, crows, and magpies and of their breeding areas. He also advocates that in areas of high vole density resting perches should be erected from which such birds could hunt.

Spain

In July 1975 routine tests revealed two rabid dogs in Malaga. For the past decade Spain had been completely free of rabies. This case is particularly interesting as it has bearing on the possibility of transmission between pets and wildlife. In total 114 cases were reported. These included 68 dogs, 45 cats, and 1 fox (Garrido 1978). One man died having been bitten by an unvaccinated (i.e. illegal) dog and then refusing post-exposure treatment after the fifth injection. The one rabid fox bit a person in Malaga in July 1977, two years after the first rabid dog was detected. Subsequent tests on wildlife have failed to find any further cases of rabies. This is disturbing evidence of a link between wildlife and pets in a country which has a lower urban population of both than does the UK.

Italy

In 1977 rabies entered the north of Italy via the Krimml Pass. Soon

after the outbreak a meeting of experts at Bolzano in October recommended that attempts should be made to reduce the fox population.

North America

Since rabies was first diagnosed in a fox in the United States in 1753 in
Virginia it has spread across much of North America. In 1819 the
Governor-General of Canada died after being bitten by a rabid fox.
From 1946 to 1966 the disease accounted for nearly 150 human deaths,
although recently through modern prophylaxis and compulsory vaccination of pets the threat to humans has been reduced to an almost
minimal level. In comparison, the figure for South America is more
daunting: over 2350 human deaths between 1954 and 1965 (Acha 1966).
The threat of the disease, which prompts widespread post-exposure
vaccination, has itself a high cost, over 30 000 people being treated
annually. In 1969 the Pan American Zoonoses Center set up a rabies
surveillance unit to study the disease over 40 million km² of the New
World, inhabited by 500 million people. By 1972 they had monitored
only 8 human cases in the USA and Canada and 774 in the 28 South
American countries. During the same period 994 rabid dogs were
reported in the northern region, and 52 993 in the south. In contrast,
12 125 wild animals were reported in the north and 803 in South
America.

In 1976, 3146 confirmed cases of rabies were reported by the US
Department of Health, of which 87 per cent were among wild animals.
Ten states reported over one hundred cases: California (357), Texas
(347), Georgia (225), Minnesota (193), Oklahoma (181), Arkansas
(155), North Dakota (137), South Dakota (114), and Florida (100). The
animals concerned were skunks (47 per cent), bats (23 per cent),
racoons (9 per cent), foxes (62), cattle (52), dogs (42), cats (32), and
horses and mules (12).

A comparison of the incidence of rabies in wildlife between America
and Europe is given in Fig. 3.11, which contrasts the proportion of cases
diagnosed in different species in France and the United States. The
situation in one state, Virginia, provides an example. From 1955 until
the early 1960s Virginia reported one of the highest incidences of fox
rabies of all states in America, and in the 1960s the problem persisted;
for example, 147 rabies-positive foxes were diagnosed in 1967 (Baker
1967). The high incidence of fox rabies prompted a State trapping
campaign, commenced in 1961, with foxes (both the red fox and
the grey fox) as the principal targets. By the late 1960s there was no
evidence that the trapping scheme had improved the situation at all.
Indeed, some opinion maintained that it had exacerbated the problem
through some improperly understood biological side-reactions.

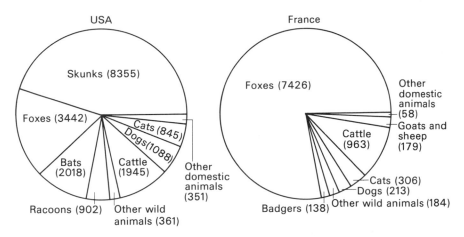

Fig. 3.11. Rabies in the USA (1969–73) (*left*) and France (March 1968–December 1975) (*right*); the numbers are of confirmed animal cases. (From Office of Health Economics 1977.)

Between 1963 and 1968 the Virginia South West District Health Laboratory investigated 2356 animals sent to them, of which 25 per cent (591) were rabies-positive; 390 of the 591 cases (65.9 per cent) were among wildlife. There are difficulties in interpreting these data which beleaguer all attempts to unravel the relative importance of different species (or wild versus domestic species) in a rabies epizooty. For example, in the Virginian study, although the majority of positive diagnoses were among wild animals, the minority of species submitted for examination by the Health Authority were wild species; that is, they made up only 39 per cent (920 out of 2356) of individuals submitted for examination. Thus, as Prior (1969) points out, something like three times as many of the wild animals investigated were positive in comparison with the domestic animals. The data from the Virginia South-west District Health Laboratory are presented in Table 3.4. They show, for instance, that the highest percentage of positive diagnoses in terms of individual tests occurred amongst bobcats (83.3 per cent) and grey foxes (67.2 per cent) in comparison with cattle (33.7 per cent) and red foxes (27.5 per cent). It is very interesting that Prior also discovered that there was a significant relationship between the number of both cats and dogs submitted to the Laboratory from the different counties within Virginia State and the distance of these counties from the Laboratory itself. She did not find, however, any such relationship with cattle. In short then, dog and cat owners appeared less willing to submit

Table 3.4   Animals submitted for rabies examination, to the Virginia Southwest District Health Laboratory, 1963–1968†

Species	Number submitted	Per cent of total submitted	Number positive	Per cent positive of submitted
Grey fox‡	524	22.24	352	67.18
Red fox	98	4.16	27	27.55
Total fox	*622*	*26.40*	*379*	*60.93*
Small rodents§	119	5.05	0	0.00
Skunk¶	36	1.53	2	5.56
Rabbits	31	1.32	0	0.00
Racoon	29	1.23	1	3.45
Woodchuck	29	1.06	0	0.00
Opossum	20	0.85	0	0.00
Bat	18	0.76	2	11.11
Shrews, moles	7	0.30	0	0.00
Bobcat	6	0.25	5	83.33
Deer	4	0.17	1	25.00
Weasel	2	0.08	0	0.00
Boar	1	0.04	0	0.00
Total wildlife	*920*	*39.05*	*390*	*42.39*
Cats	510	21.65	45	8.82
Dogs	501	21.26	35	6.99
Cattle	335	14.22	113	33.73
Misc. farm	57	2.42	8	14.04
Guinea pigs, and hamsters	28	1.19	0	0.00
Monkeys	5	0.21	0	0.00
Total domestic	*1436*	*60.95*	*201*	*14.00*
Total wild and domestic	2356	100.00	591	25.08

† Does not include animals unfit for examination.
‡ Includes four foxes not designated as to species; two were diagnosed positive.
§ Some of these were laboratory animals or pets and therefore might be considered as 'domestic' animals.
¶ Forty-one additional skunks were collected and submitted from Montgomery county as part of a survey conducted in 1967 by Mr John Beck, USFS; none was diagnosed positive.
Source: Prior (1969).

animals for examination the further away they lived from the Laboratory, while farmers appeared equally ready to submit cattle irrespective of where they lived. The grey fox composed 22.4 per cent (524 out of

2356) of the animals submitted to the Health Laboratory but it also accounted for 57.3 per cent of the positive diagnoses during these years.

Differences in interpreting such data in the light of these sample biases may include allowances made for the considerable economic value of cattle and the improbability of ever seeing a fox under normal circumstances unless it was already unhealthy. Similarly, distinguishing between the role of the red fox and the grey fox in the Virginian epizooty presents problems; more grey foxes were submitted for examination and 67.2 per cent of these were positive in comparison with only 27.5 per cent of the red foxes submitted. These figures may hide differences, not only in the population density of the two species or of their susceptibility to the disease, but also in their shyness towards men and the difficulty in trapping them. In fact Prior indicated that the proportion of red to grey foxes submitted for analysis at the Laboratory was different from the proportion of the two species killed by trappers in the State. In general, Swink (1967) believes that the grey fox is the primary vector in the south-east of the United States while the red fox is in the north-east. Considering the Virginian situation in the 1960s, Prior speculated that the rather low proportion of submitted red foxes that were rabies-positive resulted from an epizooty of mange currently affecting the red foxes which made them either more susceptible to hunters or confused people into thinking they were rabid and hence increased the number of non-rabid foxes submitted for examination.

Some of the problems of interpreting figures on human exposure to rabies are handled in two articles by a team of Illinois doctors who studied cases in that State between 1963 and 1968 (Schnurrenberger, Martin, Maedink, and Rose 1969; Martin, Schnurrenberger, and Rose 1969). They were particularly concerned that over one-third of people were vaccinated for spurious reasons, presumably just to put their minds at rest. For instance, three people were vaccinated after drinking tea made with water boiled in a saucepan used the previous day to bathe the eyes of a rabid dog. A blacksmith who shod a pony before it became rabid demanded treatment, as did his wife, who had brushed the clothes he had worn at the time. There are noteworthy differences in the incidence of rabies cases, the resulting numbers of exposure cases, and the number of people vaccinated as reported by different authors; for example, although skunks were only 2 per cent of 937 animals responsible for human vaccination, they represented 71 per cent of 347 rabid animals reported in 1967–8. They also report various sex and age differences: children were more commonly exposed to dogs and cats than adults, and almost twice as many men as women were vaccinated (see also Fig. 5 in Martin *et al.* 1969, p. 1074).

In spite of interpretative difficulties some generalizations emerge.

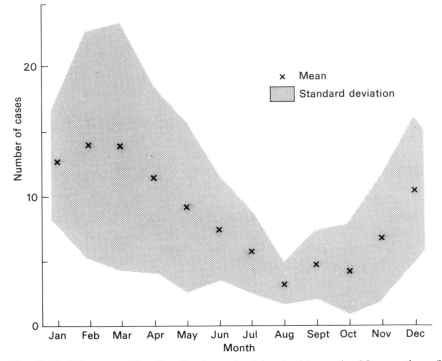

Fig. 3.12. The monthly distribution of rabies incidence in 16 counties of Western Virginia, 1963–8. (After Prior 1969.)

One, which comes from the Virginian study in close agreement with what has been described for the European situation, is the seasonal variation in the incidence of rabies. Figure 3.12 shows that the incidence dropped to a low in August from a peak in February and March. These figures refer to all cases of rabies, the majority of which were among grey foxes.

In another North American study, Johnston and Beauregard (1969) found a similar annual pattern of infection in Canadian foxes sampled in Ontario. The annual incidence of rabies in various species sampled by these researchers between August 1961 and March 1969 is shown in Fig. 3.13.

The study in Ontario is particularly interesting as, at least indirectly, it provides evidence on interactions between some of the different species infected by the disease, in particular foxes and porcupines. Rabies first appeared among wild animals in Ontario in 1954 and by 1958–9 a major epizootic had broken out among foxes which accounted for 43 per cent of the total rabies cases reported; the second most

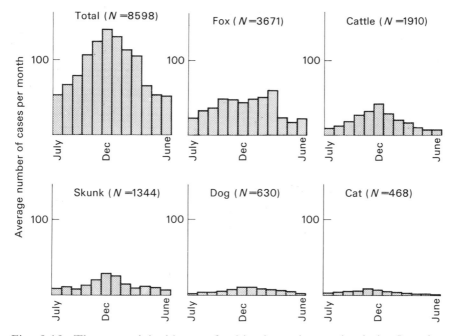

Fig. 3.13. The annual incidence of rabies in various animals in Ontario, Canada, averaged over the period August 1961 to March 1969. (After Johnston and Beauregard 1969.)

important species was the striped skunk (*Mephitis mephitis*) which constituted 16 per cent of the total of rabies cases. As Fig. 3.14 shows, Johnston and Beauregard noticed that the monthly incidence of rabies in red foxes began to increase each year before the annual peak for other species. As with the Dutch data analysed by Niewold, the Canadian study also revealed seasonal differences in the infection in different sexes. Males were much more frequently infected than females and they comprised the bulk of animals found rabid during the winter epizootic peak. However, the majority of rabid foxes during the late spring breeding season were vixens. In an attempt to reconstruct aspects of the behaviour of rabid foxes from the corpses sent to these researchers by hunters, they examined them for signs of recent scars from fighting which might have indicated injury acquired during the furious stage of rabies. Of 235 rabid foxes, 40 per cent showed evidence of what Johnston and Beauregard termed 'ferocious contact'. Apparently animals collected from areas where rabies outbreaks were particularly frequent exhibited a disproportionate occurrence of such injury. A

Fig. 3.14. A rabid fox in Ontario with its face mutilated by porcupine quills. Rabid foxes are injured in this way more frequently than more prudent healthy animals. (Photograph courtesy of D. Johnston.)

second point to emerge was that the incidence of ferocious contact appeared uniformly distributed from month to month with the exception that during March there was a significantly higher percentage of injury to the faces of vixens (80 per cent). In particular signs of contact with porcupines, which leave quills imbedded in the face of any adversary, were noted. Indeed, 34 per cent of rabid red foxes had quills in their muzzles. All these injuries seemed to be recent, indicating that such unprofitable encounters with porcupines had been entered into only after the foxes had become rabid.

The Ontario fox rabies resulted from an epizootic which began in the Arctic, reaching Ontario in 1951. Previously fox rabies had been almost unknown in the state, except for the case of the Duke of Richmond who died from the bite of an imported pet fox. Today fox rabies is rare in North Dakota (Sargeant, personal communication), but there skunk rabies is, and has long been, endemic. Skunk rabies is not a problem in Ontario. This strange situation poses the question of why does the Ontario epizootic not spread south (why, for that matter, did it first begin in the Arctic?). It seems unlikely that the Great Lakes and St Lawrence River could be an impenetrable barrier since they freeze annually. Although skunks are less mobile than foxes and known to live at rather low densities between Ontario and Dakota, it is also puzzling that skunk rabies hasn't travelled north. Paradoxes of this type are not uncommon—racoons still account for much of Florida's rabies, although other potential vectors inhabit the area. In fact, as the Arctic epizootic swept south in the late 1950s foxes in South Ontario became infected. Now however, it is only in North Ontario that the disease is endemic. Another case where rabies disappeared spontaneously is New York where a possible explanation may be sought in the fact that foxes suffered a serious epidemic of mange and distemper coincident with a massive poisoning campaign; the combined effects may have reduced the fox population below that which could sustain rabies.

The studies of Andral and his colleagues in France have recently shown indications of successive waves of rabies in areas that had pre-viously been swept by the epizootic front. This pattern has been familiar in other parts of Europe also, including Czechoslovakia (Kral 1969) and Denmark (Müller 1966). Indeed, a similar pattern emerged in some areas during the Ontario study. It is interesting that Johnston and Beauregard noted that in localities where foxes had been known to exist in relatively dense populations prior to the rabies epizooty, the period-icity of successive peaks in fox rabies was three years. They concluded that these more densely populated areas constituted optimal habitat for the foxes. In other areas which they thought to be suboptimal fox habitat, the peaks in successive waves of rabies were broader and occurred at four- or five-year intervals, and evidently involved fewer animals. Similar differences in the periodicity of rabies outbreaks have been observed in other studies: for example in Germany Kauker and Zettel (1960) noted a three-year cycle; Friend in 1968 reported a four- or five-year cycle in New York. The general conclusion is that, for both red and Arctic foxes, rabies epizooties coincide with relatively high fox population densities. This relationship with vector population density is also found in other epidemic diseases. For instance, Havlik (1954) reports peaks in Central European tick-borne encephalitis following 'mouse-years'. In Russia Myasnikov, Levacheva, and Yogiazaryan (1961) describe a peak in bank vole numbers following a good tree seed crop in 1957. This was followed by an epidemic of haemorrhagic fever.

The European rabies problem has been summarized by Wachendörfer (1977) who analysed the World Health Organization questionnaires from 1972 to 1976 and found that 22 of 32 European states were infected with an aggregate total of 96 623 animal cases and 336 human cases (of which 14 were imported). Wachendörfer recognized five patterns (their distribution is shown in Fig. 3.15):

(1) sylvatic rabies in central Europe (Fig. 3.16(a));

Fig. 3.15. The distribution of rabies in Europe, 1975–6. (After Wachendörfer 1977.)

    (2) canine rabies, in eastern and south-eastern Europe and the Mediterranean region (Fig. 3.16(b));

    (3) canine rabies plus a regional focus of wildlife rabies in south-east Europe and the USSR (Fig. 3.16(c));

    (4) Arctic rabies; and

    (5) rabies-free areas.

In the 11 central and western European countries, foxes accounted for 73.6 per cent of the reported cases (Fig. 3.15(a)). In contrast, for Italy, Spain, Turkey, Algeria, Morocco, and Greenland 77.2 per cent of the 13 477 cases were among domestic carnivores and only 0.07 per cent among foxes, wolves, or jackals (Fig. 3.15(b)). Wachendörfer's data show that 93.2 per cent of rabies cases in man (332 between 1972 and 1975) occurred in countries where canine rabies predominates (68.4 per cent of the cases were in Turkey, 15.7 per cent in Morocco, and 8.6 per cent in Yugoslavia). The ratio of recorded animal cases to the number of

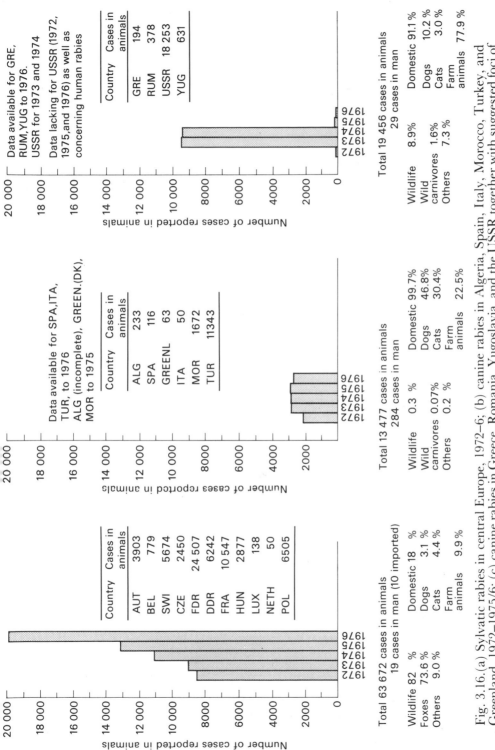

Fig. 3.16.(a) Sylvatic rabies in central Europe, 1972–6; (b) canine rabies in Algeria, Spain, Italy, Morocco, Turkey, and Greenland, 1972–1975/6; (c) canine rabies in Greece, Romania, Yugoslavia, and the USSR together with suggested foci of local wildlife rabies, 1972–6. (After Wachendörfer 1977.)

Table 3.5   The ratio between the number of cases of
rabies in animals and the number of persons treated for
the disease

Pattern	Country	Ratio
I Sylvatic rabies	Luxembourg	1:0.5
	France	1:0.8
	Switzerland †‡	1:1.1
	Belgium	1:1.3
	Czechoslovakia	1:1.3
	Netherlands	1:1.6
	Poland	1:2.6
	Hungary	1:3.7
	East Germany	1:4.4
	Austria §	—
	West Germany ¶	—
II Canine rabies	Turkey	1:19
	Algeria	1:29
	Morocco	1:32
	Spain	1:94
	Italy †	1:1632
III Canine rabies with suggested regional foci of wildlife rabies	Yugoslavia	1:19
	Greece	1:75
	Romania	1:162
	USSR §	—

Sources: Questionnaires 1972–6, Italy WHO World Surveys 1972–5;
from Wachendörfer (1977)
† Estimated figures
‡ Pre-exposure vaccination included
§ No persons treated not reported
¶ Exact data not available

post-exposure treatments in man varies enormously between different
countries (Table 3.5)—ranging from 1:0.5 to 1:1632.

These detailed descriptions of rabies epizootiology in selected regions
allow us to make several generalizations. In Europe the red fox is the
principal vector and victim among wildlife species, as it would presumably be in Britain were rabies to cross the English Channel. The
epizootic front advances into new territory rather slowly at between 30
and 60 kilometres a year but there are occasional outbreaks well in
advance of the main front. There are seasonal variations in the number

of rabid foxes encountered. There is an overall peak in the winter which predominantly involves male foxes and a subsidiary peak in the breeding season which, although of minor importance in absolute numbers, includes the majority of vixen cases. Interpretation of gross differences in species infection rates and indeed in the magnitude of an epizootic impact is bedevilled by sampling difficulties, but the statements above appear to have some generality, as does the contention that once an area has become infected the disease will recur periodically with a shorter period and more clearly defined peaks in better fox habitat.

It is appropriate now to turn to the biology of the fox and to consider its behaviour and ecology in the context of these observations on the occurrence of the disease. In the next two chapters I shall first summarize what is known of fox biology and try to link this knowledge with the behaviour of rabies epizootics. Then I shall consider the efficacy of different methods of controlling the spread of rabies through fox populations.

4   Fox biology

The fox's ubiquity has already become clear during the preceding discussion of the distribution of fox rabies. The rabies problem is almost world-wide, and the fox's geographical range is similarly expansive; the same species of fox that is familiar in the British countryside is also indigenous throughout North America and Canada and across Europe and Asia to Korea and ranges from Arctic to tropical latitudes. Clearly, with such a geographical range and diversity of habitats the red fox must be an adaptable species. This adaptability at the same time makes the fox an attractive subject for biological research and brings it into conflict with man not only through public health problems, but in many other ways as well. One factor contributing to the fox's ability to survive in such widely different habitats is its versatile hunting behaviour and catholic tastes which enable it to capitalize on a vast array of prey species.

The composition of fox diet is one aspect of the species' biology on which there is considerable information. Biologists have either collected fox faeces, and analysed them microscopically in order to identify the prey remains therein, or alternatively have examined the stomach contents of foxes brought to them by hunters. In every study one common denominator amongst the findings has been that in any one area the foxes are eating a large variety of different prey. These include species as diverse as hares and beetles, game birds and voles, or chamois and earthworms. The detailed composition of fox diet might at first seem irrelevant to the very practical problem of stemming the tide of a rabies epizootic. However, during the past couple of decades, biologists have come increasingly to view the behaviour and, in particular, the social behaviour of animals in terms of adaptations to environmental features. That is to say that an understanding of the way individuals of the species are organized and how they behave within a community can be viewed as adaptions to ecological circumstances. The epizootiology of rabies is intimately linked with the behaviour of foxes. Thus, if we are to understand this link we need to understand the behaviour of foxes and, in turn, the ecological determinants of their mode of life. Examples of links between the behaviour of individual animals within a population and their ecological circumstances have come to light recently. For example, Jarman (1974) described the social organization of a range of species of African antelopes. Of course, he noticed dramatic differences in the community structure of different species with extremes ranging from the tiny duiker which lives a rather solitary life defending its territory in wooded areas and the ponderous eland which grazes the open grass-lands in herds numbering thousands. Jarman elegantly linked the social organization of these various species to the type of food supply that each was exploiting. In this example the territorial duiker eats succulent shoots and fruits scattered throughout the woodland. These are difficult to find and so, to ensure sufficient food, the duiker must not only know the area he forages very intimately, but he must also prevent other members of his species picking the precious fruits before he can harvest them himself; hence the territorial way of life and many of its social concomitants can be traced back to the food supply. In contrast, the eland grazes on abundant, but low-quality, grass; the presence of other members of its species near by while an eland forages is not a disadvantage through interference and this leaves the way open for the eland to capitalize on other benefits of a more gregarious existence, for example having many pairs of eyes to keep alert for approaching predators. In each case again, the animal's society is linked to features of its environment, such as quality and availability of food, and the threat of predation. In this example the way the two species use space and the distances they travel are, because of their different diets, hugely diverse. If animal movement-patterns can be understood through a study of their exploitation of food resources, then this too is clearly relevant for the rabies epizootiologist concerned with the possibilities of disease transmission between different foxes.

A glance out of the window is sufficient to remind everybody that each species of animal has its own particular lifestyle; sparrows visiting the bird tables do so as a flock, while the robin comes alone. However, some of the very large differences that exist between communities of animals of the same species are less obvious. Detailed study has revealed intraspecific variation in behaviour for a number of species, in particular among the order Carnivora of which the red fox is a member. A notable example is Kruuk's (1972) study of the spotted hyaena in East Africa. Kruuk studied the details of the behaviour and ecology of this species, on the one hand to understand better the adaptive significance of hyaena social behaviour, and on the other, to use this knowledge as the foundation of a management plan for the species within the Serengeti National Park. So, in the hyaena study too, an understanding of the details of the species' behaviour was considered essential for its sound management.

Kruuk watched spotted hyaenas in two areas in the Serengeti, one of them a crater in which the prey populations were confined by encircling volcanic walls, while the other was in the open plain where the famous migrations of large African ungulates took place annually. These two districts posed very different problems for the spotted hyaena attempting to capture, for example, wildebeest, zebra, and gazelle. In the crater, the prey were relatively stable in their availability to the hunting hyaena, whereas outside on the plains the prey migrated over hundreds of miles leaving behind them impoverished areas without food for the hyaenas. There the predator was left only with the option of following the migrating herds. Consequently, Kruuk found considerable variation in the social system of spotted hyaenas in the two areas: within the crater the hyaenas lived in stable clans—matriarchal societies whose individual composition remained the same from year to year and who co-operatively defended a clearly defined territory from neighbouring clans. The territory borders were demarcated with piles of faeces and the carefully positioned secretions of a variety of scent glands which presumably proclaimed ownership of that patch. In contrast, hyaenas on the plains lived in unstable and rather small groups whose composition changed from month to month and which made no attempt to demarcate territory borders with faeces but instead utilized middens along well trodden tracks.

A popular account of this research can be found in Kruuk (1976). For our purposes the important point to note is that where individuals of a species live in different environments their behaviour may adapt in profound ways to the different ecological pressures presented by each habitat. In fact, variation in behaviour of individuals in contrasting habitats may be so dramatic that they may be scarcely recognizable as the same species on the basis of their behaviour. We know that the red fox lives in a huge variety of habitats throughout its expansive geographical range and also shows variation in its behaviour of the sort that Kruuk's study demonstrated for the spotted hyaena. It is vital for the rabies epizootiologist to understand the basis of this variation so that management schemes, whatever their nature, can be adjusted to accommodate this behavioural plasticity.

Against this background of the necessity to understand fox behaviour in the context of differing ecological circumstances, we can consider first what is known about the fox's use of space. Some information on fox movements has been gained through mark–release–recapture or ear-tagging studies. These involve marking foxes with an individually numbered tag which is subsequently recovered when the animal is shot by a hunter, killed by a car, or otherwise returned to human hands. Nothing is known about what happened between the capture point and recapture point, nor about the route taken between them. Results do, however, provide interesting 'average' figures for different aspects of fox behaviour. For instance, three American studies have each independently shown that dog foxes are, in general, killed further from the point where they were originally tagged as subadults than are vixens;

Fig. 4.1. Over much of its wide geographic range the red fox is a principal victim of vector of rabies. Few species can have intrigued so many generations of men and yet remained so poorly understood. (Photograph courtesy of J. Macdonald.)

the three respective figures being 43, 26, and 26.3 km for dog foxes and 8, 13.3, and 7.1 km for vixens. We have to seek explanations not only in the species' sociology for these sex differences, but also in the ecology of the different populations for the variation in the three studies.

The movement-patterns of foxes in Denmark are of particular interest because that country is one of the few which can boast success in controlling the rabies epizootic (as will be discussed below). Interestingly, there has also been a detailed study of the movements of ear-tagged foxes by a Danish biologist (Jensen 1968). With the aid of a dachshund, Jensen captured 460 cubs around their earths between 1965 and 1969. Encouraged by the incentive of a 50-kroner reward, Danish hunters were requested to return all ear tags collected from foxes to Jensen's research station. In this way he managed to get records on 202 cubs (i.e. 44 per cent of those that he had marked). The fate of the remaining 56 per cent of the population remains an unknown and disconcerting variable. Of those foxes recovered, 177 were shot, which gives some indication of the impact of hunters on the production of fox populations in some areas. Some studies have recorded occasional extraordinarily long treks by foxes, for example one of 257 km and another of 394 km, but as Jensen's work and that of others reveals, such enormous journeys are rare. In fact, 55 per cent of males were recovered less than 5 km from the point of marking, while the figure for vixens was 78 per cent. However, a month-by-month analysis of Jensen's figures reveals that from October to the end of the year a steadily increasing percentage of recovered subadults were found at greater distances from their natal earth. In October, 28 per cent of the dog foxes and 17 per cent of the vixens were killed more than 5 km away; during November and December the figures rose to 73 per cent and 34 per cent; and for January and February 80 per cent of the dog foxes and 31 per cent of the vixens were killed more than 5 km from their natal earth. These figures, it should be stressed, refer to foxes which were tagged as cubs. Jensen also attempted a similar study by tagging adults. However, the enormous difficulties of catching adult foxes alive meant that he tagged only 16 of them. The recovery from this small sample indicated to him that once adult the majority of foxes did not move more than 5 km from their place of capture. Excluding those foxes that were recovered within 5 km of their birthplace, Jensen has plotted the capture and recovery points for the foxes in his study. These are shown in Fig. 4.2.

Jensen's study achieved a very high rate of recovery through the severe intensity of hunting and the co-operation of hunters in returning tags. He points out that in spite of increasing shooting pressure, the number of foxes killed annually by sportsmen has continued to increase over the past 25 years from 25 000 to more than 50 000. This indicates

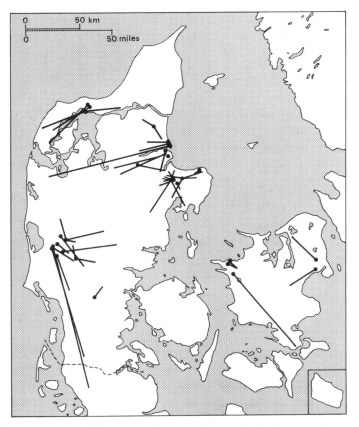

Fig. 4.2. Recoveries of first-year foxes in Denmark which moved more than 5 km from the point of tagging. The dots indicate the points of recovery. (After Jensen 1968.)

that the fox population is probably increasing in spite of culling, and raises the general question of the efficacy of hunting.†

Englund (1980) has recently studied dispersal in Sweden, tagging so far some 700 cubs and adults. Three males have been shot at 150, 200, and 220 km from their place of capture while two young vixen moved 200 and 210 km in less than 120 days. Overall, in 1975, 63 per cent of juvenile dog foxes killed had travelled more than 10 km whereas most adults and all juvenile vixens killed were within 10 km of their capture point.

Perhaps the largest-scale tagging and recovery study is that recently

---

† Throughout this text the word 'hunting' is used in the general sense to embrace shooting, gassing, poisoning, and hunting with dogs.

published by Gerald Storm and his colleagues (Storm, Andrews, Phillips, Bishop, Sineff, and Tester 1976) who, working in Illinois, Iowa, and Minnesota between 1965 and 1970, ear-tagged 2049 foxes (1987 cubs and 62 adults). Of these they recovered 807 animals from trappers. This American study reveals, as had Jensen's work in Denmark, that males generally disperse further than vixens. For animals recovered in their first year, the mean distance between first and last captures for dog foxes was 31 km; for vixens it was 11 km. This difference between dispersal by the sexes seems general to all habitats. For instance, E. Lindström (personal communication) has tagged 24 male and 17 females in the northern Taiga region of Sweden. Of his recoveries 8 males and no females had travelled more than 3 km, while 6 males and 4 females had travelled less than that distance.

Most interestingly, Storm and his co-workers collected data from different habitats throughout the three states that they studied; in particular they distinguished two ecosystems, one of them farming a strip along the Mississippi River which was relatively lush, wooded, and rolling countryside compared with the intensive farming areas more distant from the river. They found a number of indications of differences between the behaviour of foxes in these two habitats. Foxes in the open agricultural areas seemed more subject to predation by man; 40 per cent of foxes marked in the agricultural land were recovered, while only 28 per cent of those marked in the wooded areas were killed by hunters.

In contrast to the Danish study where, in spite of the efforts of hunters, the fox population appears to be increasing, there was some evidence of a decline in fox numbers in Iowa during the years covered by this project: hunting pressure certainly seems to have been severe, because 97 per cent of the tagged cubs recovered were killed during their first or second year of life, only 3 per cent being recovered from their third to sixth year. This difference possibly stems from the few opportunities for escape afforded by the barren prairies.

Figure 4.3 shows the difference in distance travelled between first and last capture for animals tagged either as cubs or adults. The columns represent the percentage of dog foxes and vixens recovered more than 8 km from their point of original release. The sample is divided into three categories: foxes tagged as cubs and recovered either in their first year or in their second year, and foxes tagged as adults. Again it appears that a much smaller proportion of animals tagged as adults move great distances. Without further information interpretation of these data is difficult. For example, in an earlier report of this Iowa study (Phillips, Andrew, Storm, and Bishop 1972) the authors noticed a relationship between the percentage of tagged foxes they recovered during the year and such factors as the amount of snowfall, which influenced the be-

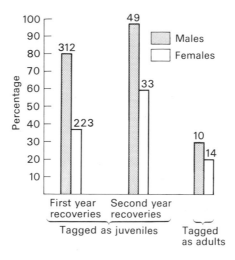

Fig. 4.3. Percentages of red foxes recovered more than 8 km from their point of release in Iowa. The number above each column is the total number of recoveries between October and March. (After Storm *et al*. 1976.)

haviour of hunters, and the price fetched by fox pelts on the open market.

Several biologists, including Storm and his co-workers, have attempted to get round these difficulties by studying in much greater detail the behaviour of individual foxes. The problem of understanding the fox's role in rabies transmission is greatly complicated because the animal is so shy and elusive and because of its nocturnal habits. For these same reasons the fox has thwarted the attempts of many biologists to probe the secrets of its behaviour. Many hours of observatons at dusk or dawn, together with miles of tracks followed through snow and sand, have served to build up a rather fragmentary picture which it has recently been possible to improve upon with the aid of radio-tracking. This new weapon in the biologist's armoury consists of a miniaturized radio-transmitter attached to the animal (in the case of the fox by a collar around its neck) which emits a pulsed radio signal. The signal can be detected at several miles' distance by a sensitive receiver operated by the biologist. A directionally sensitive aerial gives a maximum signal when the axis of the aerial is pointing at the fox, and so it is possible to plot the position of the animal from a distance. One principle for using this equipment, which I have termed *predictive* radio-tracking, attempts to combine the advantages of modern technology with the fieldcraft of

Fig. 4.4.(a) Fitting an anaesthetized dog fox with a radio transmitter in Oxford-shire. The collar is fitted with luminous and reflective material to make it easier to spot the fox by night.
(b) By stalking the radio-tagged fox (which also has been ear-tagged to display a telephone number) it is possible to observe their behaviour at close quarters in the wild. (Both photographs courtesy of J. Macdonald.)

the naturalist so that the radio apparatus is used to help the researcher to stalk close enough to the animal to watch its behaviour (Macdonald 1978*a*). I have tried to use this technique to unravel some of the mysteries in the statistics reported above in terms of individual fox behaviour.

One should remember the fox's flexibility and that it may behave in different ways in different habitats (just as Hans Kruuk's hyaenas did). To explore the limits to the flexibility of fox behaviour I have studied the species in a variety of different ecological circumstances, from deserts through suburbia to mountains (Macdonald 1977*a*).

The first conclusion from radio-tracking foxes which seems to apply to almost all habitats is that the movement data yielded by the ear-tagging studies incorporates two different sections of the fox community: one of them resident, the other itinerant. Certain foxes can be followed throughout a rather well-defined home-range† within which

† 'Home-range' is a technical term which conveniently labels that area occupied by an animal during the course of its everyday activities such as hunting, resting, and reproducing.

Fig. 4.5. Radio-tracked locations (∗) of an itinerant fox collected approximately every 15 minutes during one night. The broken lines show the boundaries of territories occupied by family groups of foxes and are based on several consecutive years of radio tracking. Territories 1 to 5 comprise principally residential habitats (e.g. gardens and orchards) whereas territory 6 is in chiefly agricultural land.

they remain for months or even years. In contrast, other foxes travelling across the same area do not follow the same consistent patterns as these resident animals, but instead move erratically over relatively large areas of land. This situation was illustrated clearly in one study area which I have investigated in detail. A map of this district is shown on Fig. 4.5. The habitat was a surburban area on the outskirts of Oxford and the behaviour of these foxes on the perimeter of a town may be particularly relevant to our understanding of the possibilities for transmission of rabies from domestic animals to wildlife species. The map shows that in even this rather small piece of land there were several resident-fox home-ranges. During the course of one night, a single itinerant fox was tracked throughout this district and radio-locations taken at fifteen-minute intervals for this fox are plotted on the same map. Not only did the itinerant cover a large area during one night, but it transgressed the borders of several of the resident-fox home-ranges. Interpreting the social significance of movements of radio-tagged foxes poses many problems (Macdonald, Ball, and Hough 1980).

Because of their erratic behaviour, radio-tracking itinerant foxes is not easy but of the 11 on which I have collected good information in this one study area, the pattern is more or less the same although there are some subtle differences between individuals. Combining the results of my own study and those of others, such as Niewold in Holland and Storm in America, it appears that the majority of subadult dog foxes become itinerant and leave the home-range in which they were born. For instance, Storm *et al.* (1976) radio-tracked five male foxes (four subadults and one adult) which yielded interesting information on dispersal. They found that with occasional detours once the young foxes had left the range they were born in, their movements had an overall direction. The males generally travelled further each night than did the females, with an average of 14.5 km per night versus 9 km per night (straight-line distance between stopping- and starting-points). These differences tally with the sex differences from ear-tagging studies mentioned above. Storm and his colleagues also noted that the speed at which the males were travelling was in general faster than that of females. One of the routes taken by a radio-tracked fox in Storm's study is pictured in Fig. 4.6(a); Table 4.1 presents the straight-line distances between the first and last point of dispersal paths for all of the foxes in Storm's study. Comparing Figs. 4.6(a) and (b), it is clear that although in my study area the itinerant fox was travelling through an enormous area compared to local resident foxes, it was covering only a tiny area in relation to dispersing foxes in the American Midwest. The habitat is very different in prairie-farming country and suburban Oxfordshire. An indication that dispersal distance is related to fox population density (which, in turn, may reflect habitat features such as food availability) can be gleaned from another ear-tagging study conducted by Lloyd (1975) in two habitats in Wales. In one of these, a sheep-farming area in the hills of mid-Wales, dog foxes were recovered an average of 10.4 km from the point where they were tagged, while females were recovered 2.2 km away. In Pembrokeshire, where the population density of foxes

Table 4.1. Straight-line distances in kilometres between first and last point of dispersal paths compared with straight-line distances between radio-tracked locations recorded throughout travel. Paths of individual red foxes

Age, Sex, State	Straight-line distance between first and last captures	Cumulative straight-line distance between consecutive radio-tracked locations
Juvenile, Male, Minnesota	62.1	102.4
Juvenile, Female, Minnesota	33.5	49.1
Juvenile, Male, Iowa	35.1	178.2
Juvenile, Female, Minnesota	31.6	58.3
Juvenile, Male, Minnesota	8.1	44.4
Juvenile, Female, Minnesota	18.2	19.0
Juvenile, Female, Iowa	6.9	25.4
Juvenile, Female, Iowa	13.2	104.3
Adult, Male, Iowa	57.5	109.1
Juvenile, Male, Iowa	13.5	18.5
Juvenile, Male, Iowa	39.1	128.6

Source: Storm *et al.* 1976.

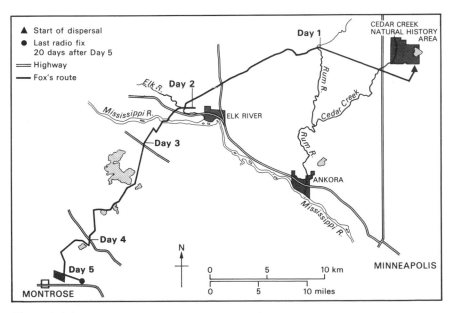

Fig. 4.6.(a) The dispersal route of a subadult male fox in Minnesota.

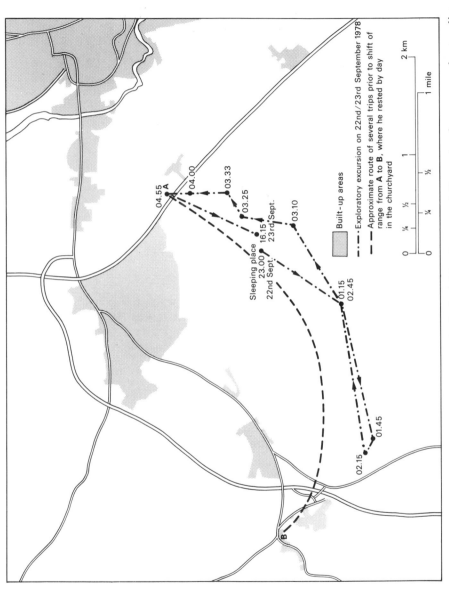

Fig. 4.6. (b) The route taken by a similar subadult male in Oxfordshire. In general dispersing foxes cover shorter distances in habitats where the fox population density is higher. (Fig. (a) after Storm *et al.* 1976.)

was apparently much higher, the respective distances for males and females were 4.6 and 1.9 km. There were other differences between the two areas: in mid-Wales 60 per cent of the population sampled were juveniles, while only 33 per cent were juveniles in the killed sample in Pembrokeshire where the home ranges were much smaller (80 ha) and foxes lived at a density of 4–5 per km² (Lloyd, personal communication). The greatest dispersal distance so far recorded in Wales for a fox cub is 53 km.

The question of what determines distance travelled by itinerant foxes is one of the aspects of fox biology most relevant to rabies control, since it is clear from Fig. 4.6 that the itinerants cover potentially much larger areas of ground than the residents. So, it seems likely that the itinerants determine the speed at which the disease can spread from individual to individual. To understand better why the itinerants† travel over shorter straight-line distances in densely populated fox habitats we must consider what features distinguish them from the resident foxes.

So far, I have termed the area utilized by resident foxes the home-range and to the biologist this term does not imply defence of an area. However, observation of radio-tagged and individually recognizable foxes within my study areas, using infrared binoculars which enable one to see at night, has demonstrated that the resident foxes defend their home-range against intruders. Technically, a defended home-range is called a territory. Territoriality is one mechanism whereby the population density of a species is adjusted to the availability of resources such as food. Each territory holder is defending sufficient resources to support itself and its family. When all the critical resources have been divided up between territories any remaining animals face little more than the prospect of starvation (or at least not breeding) until they can establish themselves in a territory that becomes vacant. This phenomenon is dramatically illustrated by certain species of birds, such as grouse, in which the majority of the population starve every winter simply because they were not successful in competition for a territory. Thus the number of young birds fledged in the summer has no bearing on the number that will be alive next spring; all those that do not get a territory to supply them with winter food will die.

While the fate of non-territory-holding itinerant foxes await further study, it seems that the fox, like so many other animal species, approximates this model of two sections of the community, those that hold critical resources and are territorial and those that do not and are

† It may become necessary to distinguish between dispersing foxes (travelling in long straight lines) and itinerant foxes (using relatively large home ranges within one district), but so far not enough is known to confirm such a distinction.

Fig. 4.7.(a) Typical fox habitat in the North of England, where rabbits, grouse, and sheep carrion are important prey and sources of food. (b) Daytime resting area of a radio-collared fox in urban Oxford. The diet here includes scraps scavenged from bird tables, garden birds, invertebrates, and animals killed on roads. The comparison highlights the fox's versatility, and this must be remembered when we attempt to control rabies. (Both photographs D. W. Macdonald.)

Fig. 4.8. Fox society is more complex than our naive attempts to summarize it suggest. Much more research, together with new interpretative frameworks will be needed before we understand the details of fox behaviour such as the 'submissive' greeting (*top*) or more aggressive fracas (*bottom*) shown here. (Photographs courtesy of D. W. and J. Macdonald.)

itinerant—put simply, the 'haves' and the 'have-nots'. Direct observations on the relationship between resident foxes and itinerants suggest that when the travelling animals are caught trespassing on a resident's territory they are attacked and expelled. Indeed, part of the erratic pattern of movements of itinerant foxes throughout my study area was determined by their flight from successive residents. Few data are yet available concerning the process of settling down or territory acquisition by itinerant animals. Perhaps their only hope is to find a territory where the resident has died or, if the resident is sufficiently feeble, they can overcome and expel it. It seems probable that the dispersal distance covered by travelling foxes is generally determined by the probability of their finding a territory in which they can establish themselves but some observations have been made of dispersing foxes travelling through unoccupied habitat. The data presented above on dispersal distances suggests that the probability of settling down varies from one habitat to the next, shorter dispersal being associated with high population density and with small territory sizes.

The size of the territory defended by resident foxes varies dramatically between different areas. For example, the mean territory size in my suburban study area around Oxford was 44.8 hectares†, while in a bleak, sheep-farming area in the north of England, the territories spanned up to 1300 ha (Macdonald 1977a). These extremes both lie outside the limits previously recorded by other studies which normally range between about 250 and 800 ha for territory size which is closer to that which I found in an agricultural habitat, again in Oxfordshire. Storm (1965) radio-tracked two male foxes which had a mean territory size of 406 ± 38 ha‡, but it is particularly interesting to note that the 54-ha difference between these two territories, which seemed trivial compared to their total area, is in fact sufficient land in itself to support more than two territories of the smallest size I have found in a suburban habitat. The intuitive explanation that territory sizes are bigger where food availability is low and thus that there is more food available around suburban Oxford than in the American prairies or the sheep country of North England, provides an adequate explanation for these observed differences. There are complications to this overly simple statement such as, for example, the pattern of food availability, overlap of territories on suboptimal habitat, and differences in range use by dominant and subordinate foxes, but these are not yet pertinent to the discussion.

It will be remembered that from year to year as the rabies epizootic has spread across Europe (Fig. 3.1, p. 14), the distance travelled by the

---

† 1 hectare = 100 m × 100 m = 10 000 sq. m = 1/100 sq. km (= 2.4 acres).
‡ Variations are expressed as standard deviations throughout the text.

Fig. 4.9. Many householders are delighted by the harmless presence of foxes in their gardens. This woman has fed the radio-collared fox pictured with her for 4 years and followed the development of the fox's cubs each spring. Such feeding sites, whether they are provided deliberately or inadvertantly (in the form of a bird table or a compost heap) are an important aspect of fox ecology in the outskirts of towns. (Photograph D. W. Macdonald.)

front varies from one area to another. One wonders whether this relates to the local habitat and thus to fox territory size.

So far I have mentioned resident foxes occupying territories without specifying how many foxes might cohabit within one territory. Some data have pointed to foxes living in monogamous pairs. Storm *et al.* (1976), for example, believe that the rather large territories in the American Midwest are usually occupied by only one adult pair of foxes joined later in the year by subadults in the form of their developing cubs, which later disperse in the way described above. However, there are some habitats in which territories support a family group of up to five or six adult foxes who live amicably together within the borders of a territory which they jointly defend. This was so, for instance, in my study area on the outskirts of Oxford. Indeed, not only does territory size vary between habitats, but so does group size. Irrespective of group size there is generally only one adult male associated with each territory. The remainder of the group consists of vixens which, the evidence suggests, are all closely related to each other. Much of the theoretical

Fig. 4.10. A vixen and her cub at close quarters. The proportion of the population of adult vixens giving birth varies widely between different habitats. (Photograph D. W. Macdonald.)

understanding of fox-group structure assumes that the resident male is the father of cubs born on his range. However, while this assumption may generally be valid, I have twice found several neighbouring males and itinerants in close proximity to an oestrous vixen. Taken together with the male's habit of making an excursion from his range during the breeding season it is possible that some resident males are cuckolded and it is likely that some sire cubs other than those in their normal territory. I have found one case, during the spring, of two adult males sharing a home-range, but I do not know what happened between them during the breeding season.

Both scientists and gamekeepers have occasionally noticed more than one adult vixen together but radio-tracking has made it possible to plot the detailed movement-patterns of each fox and demonstrates the close correspondence between home-ranges of adult vixens in the same group. The largest stable group I have studied contained six adult foxes.† Niewold has also found groups containing more than one adult vixen in some habitats in Holland and has also reported on variation in home-range size between 116–880 ha in different habitats (Niewold 1976).

† 'Popular' accounts of this work are found in Macdonald (1978*b*, *c*).

Another important facet of fox biology is reproduction. Quite a lot can be learnt about the reproductive history of individual vixens through post-mortem examination of their genital tracts. Consequently, material provided by helpful hunters has formed the basis of several major studies of reproduction within different fox populations. In particular, Jan Englund (1970) has studied 880 uteri from adult vixens collected in a variety of different habitats in Sweden. Englund's samples are large enough for him to show that there are differences in the reproductive biology of foxes in populations inhabiting different habitats. He could estimate the number of cubs each vixen had given birth to by counting the uterine scars where the placenta had attached during pregnancy. The populations in northern Sweden fluctuate drastically in different zones, while those in more southerly agricultural land are relatively stable. Englund was able to show that from year to year the birth litter sizes (at least in the north of Sweden in forested areas) varied by a factor of two—between 3.0 and 6.3. He also found a good relationship in the north between the birth litter size of a given year and the food availability measured by rodent numbers. Annual differences in food availability are particularly marked in northern habitats where rodent populations undergo large cyclical changes in their numbers (Table 4.2). Englund discovered that the total productivity (i.e. cubs per vixen per year) showed much greater annual variation than did the birth litter sizes: the sixfold fluctuations in total productivity resulted from large differences between years in the frequency of barren vixens. For example, in three successive years he found the proportion of unproductive vixens was about 35, 74, and 42 per cent. These differences, in contrast to birth litter size, did not seem directly linked to food availability since many of the barren vixens weighed about the same as

Table 4.2.   Estimated mortality rates of cubs in the northern coniferous taiga of Jämtland-Häjedalen, Sweden

Year	Percentage of cubs in the spring population	Abundance of rodents in spring–summer	Mortality rate of juvenile foxes
1967	66	Few	70
1968	29	Moderate	34
1969	56	Abundant	7

Rodents are the main prey of foxes in these areas. Prey numbers vary widely on a four-year cycle, to which vixen productivity and cub survival seem intimately linked.

After Englund (1980).

the reproductive vixens. These figures had the consequence in the northern forests of Sweden that the proportion of young animals in the population varied between enormous limits from year to year. Similar studies by Englund in more southerly agricultural regions of Sweden revealed a different situation with the vixens' productivity and the proportion of young to old animals remaining relatively constant from year to year. So, in the north, the proportion of juveniles varied between the extreme limits over four years of 21 per cent and 60 per cent of the population, whereas during a five-year period in agricultural land the extremes were 37 per cent and 46 per cent. Similarly, just as the proportion of barren vixens in the north fluctuates from year to year, so Englund has tentatively calculated the survival of cubs in the same region and suggested that this may vary from year to year between the limits of 7 per cent and 70 per cent mortality.

Englund's data are very complete but he still stresses the tentative nature of his conclusions; it remains clear from these figures that not only are there big annual reproductive differences within any one area but also between different areas. This point is further substantiated by studies from other parts of the world. For instance, in the Netherlands, F. Niewold (personal communication) found that almost all adult vixens become pregnant. Studying urban foxes in London, Harris (1978a) examined the reproductive tracts of 192 vixens whose ages he had determined. In one sample of yearling foxes Harris believes the proportion of barren vixens may have reached 52 per cent, but this was generally lower among older animals. While, as Lloyd *et al.* (1976) point out, from studied habitats in Switzerland, Bavaria and Wales about 90 per cent of vixens become pregnant. Furthermore, from a study in Wales by Lloyd, it appeared that productivity was depressed not only because of completely barren vixens, but also because in one area about 12 per cent of vixens that conceived and implanted embryos either suffered resorption or abortion or else loss of the litter shortly after birth. Lloyd *et al.* (1976) calculated the annual productivity of European foxes at a mean of 4.0 cubs per vixen, based on the assumption of a 10 per cent failure to breed, a 12 per cent loss of viable offspring, and a mean litter size of 4.7 cubs. The figure of 4 cubs per vixen may be a very useful one but the lesson of Englund's data is still to beware of considerable variation from one area to the next. Rather surprisingly, Wandeler (1976a) reports that the mean number of 4.7 cubs born per female is quite stable throughout Europe and is independent of population densities. He stresses that post-natal mortality may be more variable.

What causes these differences in the productivity of different fox populations? The observation under the unnatural circumstances of a fox farm that 37 per cent of yearling silver foxes were barren in comparison with 15 per cent of two-year-old vixens is hard to interpret in terms of the fox's natural behaviour (Pearson and Bassett 1946). More recently, it has been possible to go some way in answering this question by studying in detail the personal history of individual foxes within wild family groups (Macdonald 1979*b*, 1980). In a habitat where group size averaged between four and five adult foxes, direct observation revealed that more than half of the adult vixens did not reproduce and in some groups only one vixen reared cubs. An experimental study involving six years of observations of captive groups of foxes within enclosures complemented the data from the wild animals and confirmed that within family groups only the minority of vixens produce cubs. The breeding vixens were generally the most dominant animals within the group. In fact it seemed that a vixen's ability as a mother from one year to the next was greatly influenced by her current social status. This leads to the conclusion that, at least in habitats favouring a group size of more than two, social factors influence vixen productivity more immediately than food availability. In fact the behaviour of non-reproductive, subordinate vixens also changed with the birth of the dominant's cubs. The subordinates behaved in a very 'maternal' way towards the cubs, guarding them and carrying food to them just as diligently as the real mother. Clearly, fox social life has complex adaptations to circumstances where social factors regulate birth-rate. The mechanism of social suppression of reproduction of subordinate vixens is still uncertain.

So far the social organization of foxes in his Swedish study areas remains largely unknown, but Englund (personal communication) believes that a similar social mechanism of population regulation may well underlie his results as well as those obtained in Oxfordshire. Again, a cautionary note concerning flexibility is apposite, for it seems that in Holland the large majority of adult vixens become pregnant but there is a very high loss of cubs soon after birth, which can act to produce annual fluctuations in productivity in the Dutch study areas (Niewold, personal communication). In my own enclosure studies subordinate vixens are never even mated. The possibility must thus be acknowledged that there are two different socially mediated mechanisms concerned with fox population regulation; if this were so, it would be of critical importance to know what features of the environment determine which mechanism is operative.

It is apparent that several different processes, acting independently or in concert, could contribute to differences in fox population productivity, annual rate of turnover, and young-to-old ratios. For instance, the proportion of itinerant vixens versus territory holders, the size of fox groups occupying territories within a given habitat, and the degree to which relationships between vixens within each group were polarized into a hierarchy probably influence the stringency of reproductive repression within the group and variations, for reasons as yet unknown, in the survival of cubs in the first few days of life. Some recent observations (Macdonald 1979*b*, 1980) suggest that where more than one vixen does breed within a fox group, other social mechanisms sometimes come into play to reduce the overall productivity. For instance, in one case where two temporarily equal-ranking vixens bred within a captive group one soon attained dominance over the other, whose nervous behaviour led to the death of her cubs. Further work is needed to discover whether such behaviour occurs in the wild, where it is already known that dominant females in groups of other species of carnivore, such as wolves or dingoes, will kill the cubs of their subordinates. However, I have seen several cases of two breeding vixens rearing cubs in the same territory, and sometimes in the same earth.

A comparison of habitats where some information of fox-group sizes exists led me to hypothesize (Macdonald 1977*a*) that habitats with spatio-temporally 'patchy' prey-availability might favour larger groups and that larger groups with associated social influences on vixen reproduction might in turn explain some of the variation in vixen productivity observed between studies. For example, when food became temporarily abundant extra vixens could be recruited into the group, and their non-breeding would thus depress overall vixen productivity. When food became short supernumerary vixens could be expelled from the bottom of the hierarchy as conditions worsened. I have demonstrated this point experimentally with tame, but free-ranging, radio-collared foxes, whose status was known. These foxes were fed partly on provisioned food and by reducing the supply of this food, it was possible to produce excursions from her normal range in the more subordinate vixen, apparently as a consequence of suddenly heightened aggression by the dominant as available food dwindled.

Annual fluctuations in vole populations in the South Taiga of Sweden have provided an opportunity to test aspects of this hypothesis and so far they appear consistent with the data (Lindström 1980). One common-sense point which is easily forgotten in studying foxes collected by hunters is that the sample represents the animal's dying, and not those remaining in the population. Depending on the hunting method, the sex and age ratios of foxes in the sample may say more about the naïvety or state of hunger of the victims than it does about the real population structure of the foxes that avoided being sampled.

5 Rabies control schemes in the context of fox behaviour

So far I have presented features of rabies epizootics and of the behaviour of the red fox separately. I shall now try to combine these two in an attempt to uncover ideas on methods of controlling the disease.

Working in Baden-Württemberg in West Germany, Moegle *et al.* (1974) have attempted to explain the monthly incidence of rabies cases in terms of fox biology. They mapped all fox rabies cases recorded in the study area between 1963 and 1971, and calculated the month-by-month progression of the front. During this period 2822 fox cases were recorded. The minimum incidence of rabies and its minimum rate of spread were during May, June, and July. In February and March both these measures increased. However, in August the movement of the front accelerated although the incidence of rabies declined. In fact, between June and December the number of cases of rabies reported among foxes was lower than between January and March, but because of the distance between successive cases was greater, the front progressed faster during the second period of the year. This is shown in Fig. 5.1, which plots the average monthly distance of advance of the epizootic front and also the maximum distance of new cases during any one month from the front of the preceding month. The figure shows clearly that it was only during May, June, and July that the distance between the front and new cases was minimal, namely 5 km. During the rest of the year it varied between 10 and 20 km. In fact Moegle *et al.* show that throughout the entire year

Table 5.1. Comparison of rabies incidence and the rate of advance of the enzootic front in three areas of West Germany with different estimated fox populaton densities

	Zone A	Zone B	Zone C
Number of foxes killed per square kilometre and per year	0.7	1.1	1.5
Rabies incidence per square kilometre and per year	0.044	0.051	0.065
Average monthly progression of enzootic front (km)	4.98	4.71	4.70

Source: Moegle *et al.* 1974.

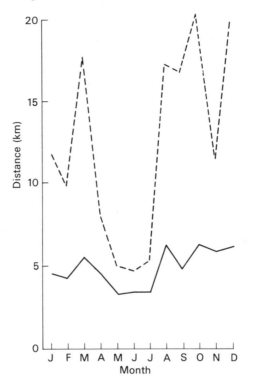

Fig. 5.1. The average monthly distance of advance of the rabies epizootic (solid line) and the greatest distances between new cases of rabies and the epizootic front of the preceding month (broken line) in Baden-Württemberg, West Germany. (After Moegle *et al.* 1974.)

93.4 per cent of new cases occur within 10 km of the previous monthly front.

An exciting discovery of this study is shown in Table 5.1 Moegle and his colleagues have categorized their data into three habitat zones of increasing fox density in West Germany. The data show that while the incidence of rabies increases from zone A to zone C with the increasing fox populaton density, the mean monthly advance of the epizootic front remained remarkedly constant between zones. That is to say that the speed with which the epizooty swept through an area, at least within the range of population densities studied by these authors, was not directly related to variations in fox density. Interpretation of this finding is complicated by the possible local variations in fox density in any given area and thus, presumably, varied opportunities for contact. For instance, a high population density might occur with small territories and small group size, or with larger territories with larger group size, and these two extremes might manifest different epizootiological characteristics. The incidence of rabies is related to density of foxes, but since the hunting indicator of fox density is probably not linearly related to real fox density, one cannot test whether incidence is directly proportional to densities.

In the face of inadequate basic data Montgomery (1974) has attempted to simulate (with a computer) the movements of foxes to discover what rate of contact might be expected under different conditions between animals moving in the same area. The idea behind a computer simulation is to 'ask' the machine to imitate the known behaviour of the fox according to a number of rules which the programmer has chosen. One then hopes that the simulated behaviour will suggest aspects of the animal's behaviour which were not previously known. In Montgomery's study a sample of the movement patterns of a wild fox was analysed disclosing such details as the average speed with which the animal moved, the duration of bursts of movement, and the frequency with which it turned and travelled in a given direction. The computer was programmed to make its simulated fox follow the same movement rules within the limits of a number of other constraints chosen on the basis of knowledge of fox behaviour. For instance, Montgomery programmed his simulated foxes in such a way that they tended to go towards places that were within 240 metres of other places which had been visited 5 or more times previously. The simulated fox ended up on the map at a location which was nowhere near such a favoured site; it was programmed to move in a direction which tended towards the centre of an elliptical home-range. This was a sensible rule since the behaviour of wild resident foxes involves repeated use of a clearly defined area. Montgomery's programming rule constrained the behaviour of his simulated fox to make it unlikely to leave its home-range. The idea of such a simulation is that if the behaviour of the simulated fox can be made to correspond more and more to that of real foxes, then the simulated fox may shed light on unknown aspects of wild-fox behaviour. Of course, the simulated behaviour may be quite unnatural but it may have heuristic value in alerting field workers to possibilities that they had previously ignored. (For a mathematical treatment, see Mollison (1977) and for a general treatment of epidemiology see Bailey (1975).)

The probability of a rabid animal meeting healthy ones could theoretically be computed (ignoring differences in the rabid fox's behaviour, stemming from the disease). Through sounds and smells, the animals can communicate across large distances and for a considerable period of time. Considering vocalizations, Montgomery programmed his simulated foxes to bark at set intervals (for instance, every 25 minutes) and

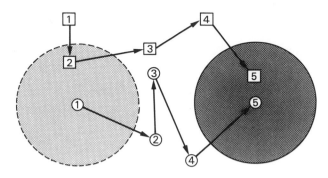

Fig. 5.2. Montgomery's simulation of the movements of foxes: the operation of the vocal communication model. The shaded circles represent the distances over which barks can be heard (e.g. from 1 and 5). As the two computer foxes move from position 1 to position 5 they eventually come within earshot of each other at move number 5. (After Montgomery 1974.)

he also specified that a fox could hear the bark of another when they were within an arbitrary distance of each other. The system is shown schematically in Fig. 5.2 where the barking fox is indicated by circles and the listening fox by squares. The position of the fox every 5 minutes is indicated successively by numbered squares or circles. Thus, if the signaller is barking every 25 minutes he barked at position 1 and position 5. The first bark, at position 1, occurred when the receiver was out of range (the receiver moved to position 2, which would have been in range, 5 minutes too late) but the second bark at position 5 occurred when the two foxes were within range. Realistic distances and responses can be incorporated into the programme as they are eventually discovered by field workers. Similar rules could be set up for visual and scent communication and other variables between habitats, sexes and ages could all be incorporated into the model. So far only preliminary explorations have been made in this potentially fruitful field.

Montgomery's model already heralds discoveries of the sort that might be relevant: Fig. 5.3, for instance, shows the simulated estimate of meetings between pairs of foxes which bark at different frequencies and have increasing vocal ranges. The distance over which the bark carries is given in kilometres and the percentage of contacts between pairs of foxes with increasing vocal carrying power is shown, depending on the frequency with which they bark (0.33 and 6.0 per hour). Montgomery's three-dimensional representation of these data (Fig. 5.4) illustrates how communication can be achieved by a variety of different combinations of vocal carrying power and frequency of vocalization. These answers are, of course, not in the least surprising and might prompt the cynic to

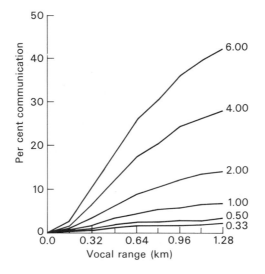

Fig. 5.3. The graph shows the effect in Montgomery's model of changing the vocal range of simulated foxes on the level of communication between them during six different cases when the simulated foxes barked at frequencies ranging from 0.33 to 6.0 barks per hour. (After Montgomery 1974.)

mutter 'so what?' This method is important because the appropriate basic information for simulating answers may soon be gathered. Even if barking is not the critical factor, understanding its influence on fox contact rates may be crucial to an appreciation of fox biology and rabies transmission.

One computer simulation study which has already unearthed surprising hypotheses about rabies transmission is Eric Preston's (1973). Preston simulated the spread of rabies through the fox population using a programme which incorporated much of the data then available on fox behaviour. So, for instance, pairs of adult foxes were assumed to occupy non-overlapping home ranges measuring 259 to 777 hectares. These pairs were assumed to breed in March with mean litter sizes of 4.59 ± 1.56 for adult vixens and 4.16 ± 1.52 for yearling vixens (although the model assumes that members of a pair only meet by chance, and not specifically at the den). The cubs of the year were not assumed to be part of the rabies susceptible population until October when they were allowed to disperse over distances which, according to their sex, were drawn from the data on dispersal distance recorded in

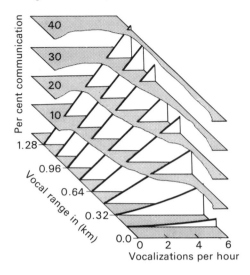

Fig. 5.4. The extent of vocal communication that occurs in five simulated pairs of red foxes with vocal ranges of 161 to 1287 m and which bark at frequencies ranging from once per 1½ hours to once every 10 minutes. (After Montgomery 1974.)

Phillips's study mentioned above. The simulation map of fox territories was divided into a number of grids containing subpopulations of foxes. The tendency to immigrate from a particular peripheral subpopulation was assumed to be directly proportional to the density differential between this subpopulation and a more central one. The 'sucking' of dispersing animals into relatively underused areas is a reasonable assumption for the model (if the habitat is uniform between the grids), reflecting the phenomenon known as 'biological vacua' to which I shall return below. Dispersing animals were moved in one of eight random directions (e.g., north, north-east, east, south-east, and so on) and they ultimately settled in the subpopulation with the lowest population density in the vicinity.

Only furiously rabid foxes were 'allowed' to pass on the disease and 50 per cent of rabid foxes were assumed to manifest furious signs. Each furious fox was assumed to travel between 20 to 35 miles during the period when signs were manifest, but the model did not investigate the effect of otherwise altering the behaviour of rabid foxes. Dispersing foxes were otherwise assumed to travel about 16 km a day. Parker and Wilsnack (1966) among others have suggested that the mean incubation period for rabies in foxes is about one month, and Preston assumed incubation after infection. In his model he started the simulation by filling each of his grid squares with 8 adult pairs of foxes occupying an average home-range of 811 hectares (by Canadian standards a rather high density). Then, choosing the north-west corner of his map, he 'infected' half the foxes in one locality (measuring 3 × 3 grid squares) with rabies (so that 3.7 per cent of the total population was infected). Using given variables he then followed the dynamics of this hypothetical population as the disease spread through it. The proportion of individuals actually contracting rabies from a furiously rabid fox passing through their home range was determined before each 'run' of the simulation. By varying this proportion, he made the progress of the disease through the population change in interesting ways.† He found that when the proportion of furiously rabid foxes was set at 50 per cent the disease could persist in the fox population only within a narrow range of values for the probability of a healthy fox being infected by the passage of a rabid fox through its range. That is, when less than 1 in 200 came in contact with a furiously rabid fox the disease rapidly died out. However, where the proportion contracting the disease was set at 1 in 40, a severe epizootic spread through over 90 per cent of the simulated population during its first year. Under these circumstances the population crashed so seriously that too few susceptible foxes were available at the end of the year to perpetuate further the infection and the disease died out. These two extremes are both shown in Fig. 5.5(a) and (d), as are graphs showing changes in the number of foxes and the number of infected foxes when the proportion of those contracting rabies was set at other intermediate values. For example, when the probability of infection was 1 in 66 (Fig. 5.5(c)) cyclical rabies outbreaks occurred during which mortality almost exactly balanced the influx of foxes through annual reproduction. The resulting density of foxes under these circumstances was about 1 per 3 square miles.

When 1 fox in 50 contracted the disease (Fig. 5.5(b)), the population crashed during the first outbreak and required two years before it had built up to a large enough size again for another outbreak to occur. These last two patterns, the one-year cycle and the three-year cycle, mirror very closely the findings for real rabies outbreaks in Northern America and Europe respectively, although they are based on runs of quite short duration (for example, 5 years).

† It is not clear whether these rabid foxes 'met' a constant percentage of the foxes in the area they travelled through; it would not seem realistic to expect this. Rather, if the rabid animal traverses a square with 20 foxes it might meet 10, but if it walked through a square with 2 it would probably miss both. P. Bacon (personal communication) suggests that a realistic formula would be:

$$\text{Number of contacts} = \text{Constant} \times \text{Density of healthy foxes} \\ \times \text{Density of rabid foxes}$$

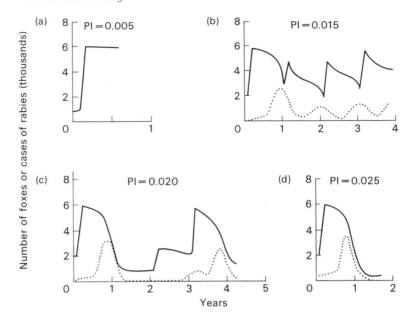

Fig. 5.5. Preston's computer simulation of fox population dynamics and rabies incidence. The index P1 corresponds to the proportion of animals contracting rabies in each area crossed by a fox infected with the furious form of the disease. The solid lines represent the total number of foxes in the population and the broken lines the number of cases of rabies. (a) The disappearance of rabies; (b) an annual cycle of rabies; (c) a self-maintained rabies cycle of 3 years; and (d) the progress of a severe epizootic and disappearance of rabies. (After Preston 1973.)

During the same simulation Preston not only followed the incidence of rabies in his hypothetical population month by month, but also the spread of the disease across his grid map. He found that when the risk of infection was set at 1 in 66 the disease spread at roughly 90 km per year. Again, there is only an approximate correspondence between this result and those from real life.

These differences were all produced by manipulation of one variable, namely the proportion of animals in a given grid square that were infected during the passage of furiously rabid foxes through that square. A number of different behavioural components are undoubtedly in-corporated into this figure. For example: the tendency of either the rabid fox, or the healthy one whose range is being invaded, to seek each other out and thereafter to attack each other; how this tendency may vary between animals of different sexes and social statuses; and indeed from season to season. It is known, for example, that where several vixens participate in one group, the more dominant animals play a greater role in territorial defence (Macdonald 1977*a*). But, for the most part, evidence on what factors actually influence the rate of contact and subsequent behaviour between rabid and healthy foxes, are little more than anecdotal.

Field data are slowly accumulating which can be incorporated into ever more realistic models which then, hopefully, have greater predictive or interpretative power. For example, contact rates and probabilities of meetings between different statuses of foxes in given habitats can be discovered in the wild and then used in models, but such data are few. Fig. 5.6 shows an example from my study area on the outskirts of Oxford where the distances between a dog fox and a vixen each time they were located have been used to estimate their probability of being in contact at any given moment. Of course, ideally one would not estimate these factors, but would measure them directly. Unfortunately, the difficulties of field studies are such that this is a slow process, although in the long run such measurements will be available (see Macdonald, Ball, and Hough 1979, for further details). Incidentally, the home-ranges of these two foxes were particularly small (approx. 10 ha) during the month (January) when the locations plotted on Fig. 5.6 were gathered.

Preston made unexpected findings in connection with the peak incidence of rabies in late winter and early spring, which was thought to relate to increased contact between individuals during the dispersal and the mating periods. The computer allows the programmer to dissect out different components that may be contributing to the behaviour of the simulation model. When Preston did this, completely omitting juvenile dispersal from the simulation (so that movement of foxes out of their home-range was caused solely by the movements of rabid individuals), he still found the same seasonal pattern of rabies incidence. He thus raised the possibility that the winter peak in rabies is nothing more than a coincidence with juvenile dispersal. Preston cautiously points out that a critical assumption on his part is that furiously rabid foxes are covering between 50 and 90 km during the period when they are shedding virus. If this assumption is high, it would anyway severely reduce the effect of dispersal. But if this assumption holds, then the annual peak in rabies incidence can be explained purely by the threefold increase in the susceptible population after July when, in the model, cubs of the year were assumed to begin participating in transmission of the disease. By January, infection with rabies had reduced the number of susceptible animals sufficiently to herald another decrease in the transmission rate.

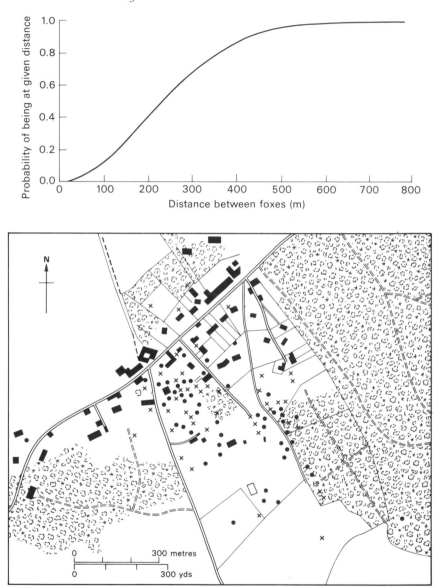

Fig. 5.6. (a) A graph of the probability that two foxes (whose ranges are shown on the map (b); × denotes a male and ● denotes a female) will be within given distances of each other. For example their probability of being within 30 m of each other is about 1 per cent ($p = 0.01$). This means they might be that close for 5–6 minutes during a long winter's night. It is then critical to know how these minutes are distributed (a dozen fleeting encounters a night, or perhaps a long meeting every week) and our evidence suggests several meetings each night.

Table 5.2.   The percentage of barren females at various
estimated population densities in New York

Region	Percentage of barren females	Index of population density means for 1951–2
Northern	16.6	0.027
Lake Plain	2.1	0.018
Southern	2.1	0.020

Source: Layne and McKeon (1956).

Preston did not show that the peak of *spatial* spread of rabies in autumn
was unaffected if dispersal is omitted.

Similarities between the behaviour of real populations and that of
Preston's simulated animals makes his model attractive. Many of the
proportions and probabilities incorporated into such simulations are
admittedly averages of populations and are little understood in terms of
the biology of the individual animals comprising them. Nevertheless,
successive versions of such models and their redesigned descendants can
incorporate more and more realistic information as it becomes available
and in so doing artefacts caused by the model's naïvety can be excluded.
Indeed, Preston included many refinements which I have not considered
here, although one more deserves mention. Using data such as that
published by Englund (1970) and Layne and McKeon (1956) on the
percentage of barren females in given populations, Preston found a
relationship between the proportion of barren animals and the density
of foxes per square mile.† Table 5.2 shows how in Layne and McKeon's
study the percentage of barren females varied with an (unproved) index
of population density such that more females were barren in heavily
populated areas. Thus, in his simulation, when the population density
of foxes in a given grid square increased, so Preston increased the
proportion of barren vixens amongst them.

This relationship is inevitably a gross oversimplification, since, as
mentioned above, my data indicate that while the proportion of barren
vixens may, indeed, be the consequence of a density-dependent process
(that is, their proportion increase with increasing population density),
this relationship is not a simple one and is confounded by the independent variations in both territory size and group size in relationship to
different habitats. Indeed, a criticism of many models of fox rabies is

† The percentage of barren females = 3.62 × (*Number of square miles/Pair of foxes*) − 22.94,
using data from Layne and McKeon summarized in Table 5.2.

that most plausible results are from long-term simulations (asymptotic), while the short-term action of the model is hard to understand (see also Smart (1970) and Smart and Giles (1973)).

Although it does not relate specifically to fox rabies, a model developed by Frerichs and Prawda (1975) bears some similarities to Preston's and illustrates another context in which computer simulations may help in the achievement of rabies control. Frerichs and Prawda (1975) were concerned with the control of rabies in the city of Cali, Colombia. In particular they wished to devise a policy which would control the disease amongst domestic dogs, but they also considered the infection of dogs by wild species. At the outset they acknowledged that a campaign of 'canine euthanasia' would be politically unacceptable in Colombia. Instead they considered the efficacy of various canine vaccination schemes, noting that after a successful vaccination programme the risk slowly increases again as old immune dogs die and young susceptible ones are born. They programmed their model to consider such subtleties as the fact that more prosperous districts within Cali accommodate dogs with a lower birth- and death-rate than those in impoverished suburbs. Also significant from a practical viewpoint was the incorporation into the model of parameters relating to the financial cost of various measures. In a poor city of 800 000 people and 84 000 dogs the expense of a control scheme is crucial.

Just as Preston included each of the variables known to influence fox biology in his model, so Frerichs and Prawda analysed those relevant to urban dog populations. All the dogs in the simulated population were either susceptible, immune, incubating, infective, or dead and the proportion in each class varied among 116 suburbs (barrios) within the town. Each barrio measured about 50 ha. A variable number of vans staffed by dog vaccination teams roamed the town and their pattern of activity influenced the proportion of dogs which were transferred from the susceptible to the immune class. However, the number of susceptibles was influenced by the birth of puppies and by the rate of decay of the immunity bestowed by the vaccine. The rate of loss of immunity depends on the vaccine used and this was also considered. All the while both immunized and susceptible dogs continue to die of other diseases irrespective of the progress of the simulated rabies outbreak. The sequence of events simulated by these authors is displayed in Fig. 5.7. The probability of a new rabid dog in a barrio is dependent on the number of infective dogs compared to susceptible ones and the rate of contact between them. Each day for which a rabid dog survived the model 'allowed' it to move either within the same or into a barrio adjacent to that which it travelled the previous day. The effects of altering these movement probabilities were not reported. In summary, the model was

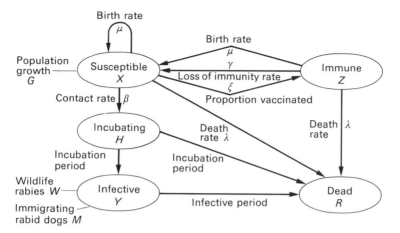

Fig. 5.7. Frerichs and Prawda's epidemiological model of the interactions and states of canine rabies. (After Frerichs and Prawda 1975.)

sensitive to variations in vaccination schedule, the number of vaccination teams, and the number of rabid dogs and wild animals.

Frerichs and Prawda ran simulations of the possible outcome of four different vaccination schemes: in one case 70 per cent of the dogs were vaccinated in the first year of an epizooty; in a second simulation a further 70 per cent were vaccinated again five years later; in a third scheme two men toured the town continuously for ten years following a schedule determined by moment-to-moment risk in each barrio. These options were compared with the cost of not vaccinating at all. In comparing the efficacy of each scheme the authors required some measure of cost. The most useful index is the cost-per-rabid-dog-prevented rather than the more conventional cost-per-dog-vaccinated, which takes no account of the effectiveness of the programme. Figure 5.8 compares the results of these options, and Table 5.3 lists the comparative costs. In the absence of such a simulation model there is no prediction of the number of cases prevented, and so no realistic method of costing.

A 70 per cent initial vaccination reduces the incidence of canine rabies for about five years, after which the annual incidence soars above that simulated when no vaccination was done at all. It is well known that diseases suddenly appear as epidemics in areas where they have been held at bay, and so the model mirrored the real world in this respect. Nevertheless (Table 5.3) the 70 per cent campaign prevented 2985 dogs (21 588 minus 18 603) from contracting rabies over 10 years. To achieve this level of vaccination the simulation had 48 men travelling in 8 trucks for 85 days and vaccinated 59 323 dogs. The theoretical cost

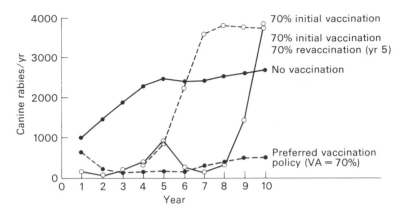

Fig. 5.8. Frerichs and Prawda's simulation of the effects of different vaccination policies on the mean number of rabid dogs per year over a 10-year period and under three different vaccination regimes. VA = percentage vaccinated in each barrio that was visited. (After Frerichs and Prawda 1975.)

Table 5.3.   Comparison of four vaccination policies, over a ten-year period, with regard to the mean cumulative number of rabid dogs, the total number of vaccinated dogs, and the cost of the individual policies.

				Cost (dollars)		
Vaccination policy	Number of epidemic trials per experiment	Mean total rabid dogs	Total dogs vaccinated	Total†	per dog vaccinated	per rabid dog prevented
No vaccination	100	21 588	0	0	0	0
70% initial vaccination (entire city) ‡	100	18·603	59 323	22 157	0.37	7.42
70% initial vaccination 70% revaccination (yr. 5) (entire city) §	10	7711	139 638	60 184	0.43	4.34
Preferred vaccination policy (VA = 70%) ¶	10	3197	100 282	64 982	0.65	3.53

† The cost of vaccination is annually increased by an inflation factor of 5 per cent.
‡ The simulated campaign took 85 days and required the use of 8 trucks and 48 vaccinators.
§ The initial simulated campaign took 85 days and the second simulated campaign, due to the canine population growth, took 112 days. Both campaigns required the use of 8 trucks and 48 vaccinators.
¶ The policy required the continuous use of 1 truck and 2 vaccinators.
Source: Frerichs and Prawda 1975.

of such an exercise would be over \$22 000 which means that each dog which was spared from rabies cost \$7.42. In comparison the cost of the double campaign was almost triple (over \$60 000), but the cost per rabid dog prevented is much less (\$4.34), since over 10 years the cumulative number of rabid dogs is reduced.

In the course of running these simulations Frerichs and Prawda hit upon a third strategy which involved two vaccinators travelling the town continuously in one truck. They moved from barrio to barrio according to the risk of rabies in each.† This scheme not only reduced the incidence of canine rabies but it was also cost-effective. Over the 10-year period, and assuming that anything between 30 and 80 per cent of the public were co-operative, the cost per prevented rabid dog remained at below four dollars (although the cost per dog vaccinated was high). The results of this study were enlightening in that the recommended vaccination strategy was by no means intuitively obvious. One might compare this approach to dogs to that in Madrid in 1763 when 900 were killed in one day in an attempt to eliminate rabies!

Figures published in 1972 by the World Health Organization show how fox populations can be limited by rabies. Figure 5.9 shows changes in the incidence of rabies in an area of 3000 km² in Baden-Württemberg in West Germany. The annual number of rabid foxes found per 10 km² can be seen to vary with the number of foxes killed by hunters per km² in the same region. As rabies began to spread through the population, the index of density measured by the hunters' success fell dramatically. The decline in fox numbers was perhaps enhanced by the introduction of earth-gassing procedures in 1964, which continued until 1966 although in that last year, the procedure was incomplete. Thereafter with the cessation of gassing and passing of the epizootic, the hunters' bag began to increase again. Simultaneous rabies 'control' by killing foxes and fox population decline due to deaths from rabies make it very difficult, if not impossible, to distinguish between different models of rabies spread.

One feature of rabies epizootics is that fox density is reduced through

† The risk was calculated for each barrio by

$$R_{i,t} = C_i X_{i,t} + \frac{1}{5} \sum_{j=1}^{5} C_{i(j)} X_{i(j),t},$$

where $R_{i,t}$ is the index of rabies risk for the barrio i at time t,
C_i relative proportion of barrio i dogs typically on the streets;
$X_{i,t}$ number of susceptible dogs in barrio i at time t;
$i(j)$ risk in five neighbouring barrios ($j = 1 \ldots 5$) to which rabid dog might travel after infection.

All these data could be continuously collected by the vaccinators as they travelled the town so that risk estimates were always up to date.

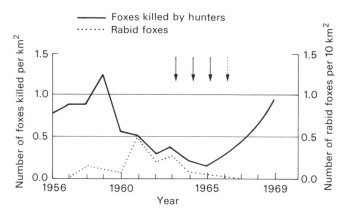

Fig. 5.9. Changes in fox population density index and incidence of rabies in the northern part of Baden-Württemberg, West Germany. The solid arrows indicate gassing campaigns; the broken one indicates an incomplete gassing operation. (After Wandeler *et al.* 1974*c*.)

disease or intensified hunting, or both. This change in population density, however it is reflected in social organization, must itself influence the transmission of the virus. Toma and Andral (1977) provide a simplified model of the transmission of a rabies virus within two fox populations of different densities. They point out that at low population densities the territory of each fox may be larger than in a zone of high population density (they ignore variations in group size). Hence they propose a model considering transmission of the virus between neighbouring territory holders in which a fox will transmit the virus farther in a low-density zone than in a high-density zone as a consequence of the average distance between nearest neighbours in the high-and low-density areas. They also suggest that the greater the number of foxes in an area the longer the virus will take to cross that area because of the increased number of relays. (The incubation period acts as a buffer of approximately one month's duration to the passage of the disease.) Toma and Andral's model is shown in Fig. 5.10. The most important conclusion that they draw from their model is that a reduction in the fox density does not automatically bring about a deceleration in the progress of the rabies front. The number of foxes in an area may nevertheless influence their encounter rate and hence the incidence of the disease might be proportional to the fox density (irrespective of the speed with which the epizootic spreads). Of course, while the speculations of these authors may be quite congruent with the observed facts, that is not

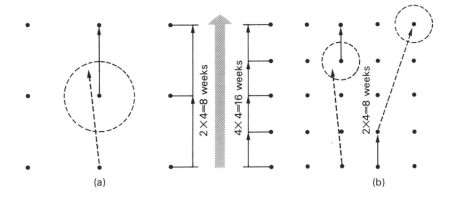

Fig. 5.10. Toma and Andral's model of the transmission of the rabies virus (a) in a fox population of low density and (b) in one of high density. Each dot represents the centre of each hypothetical fox's territory. The open arrow shows the main direction of the rabies enzootic. Viral transmission over a 4-week period is shown by a solid arrow for that between neighbours and a broken arrow for that from an itinerant fox. (After Toma and Andral 1977.)

necessarily because the system works in the way proposed by their model. For example, it is not known what proportion of rabies infections actually occur between nearest neighbours; the critical figure for this question is the mean distance travelled by a furiously rabid fox while shedding virus. It is also unknown how a furiously rabid fox is influenced, or perhaps deflected, by encounters with healthy animals. This could affect the straight-line distance travelled through areas of different fox population density. Similarly, the increased number of relays in a dense population might not result in a deceleration of the epizootic front since many more animals might be infected, hence increasing the probability of one travelling in a furious state over long distances irrespective of population density.

This is all speculation, of course. More data are needed, especially about the frequency of contact between foxes from the same and neighbouring groups. Sykes-Andral (1976) has studied reports on the behaviour of 1087 rabid foxes. One was seen fighting with another fox, one with a hare, and 20 were reported to bite anything in their paths; many showed a tendency to approach dogs.

Available evidence suggests that below a certain fox density the probability of a rabid fox encountering and infecting a healthy one is so low that the disease does not spread.† Much debate has centred around what this critical population density is and whether it can be achieved by artificial population reduction. The World Health Organization has tentatively suggested that the transmission of the disease is checked at population densities of less than one fox per 500 ha. Furthermore, in the search for generalizations, researchers have speculated that in many areas an artificial reduction in the fox population of at least 75 per cent would be required to achieve this density.

These considerations of the necessary reduction deal with rabies in Europe where the fox is generally considered the most important vector. The epizoological situation is quite different and greatly complicated in areas such as the USA by the presence of other vectors. For instance, Fischman and Young (1976) note that fox rabies recurs in geographically discrete areas. In particular they mention the Appalachian chain and the mountain ranges of Kentucky, Tennessee, Virginia, and Texas. Developing an idea of Frederickson and Thomas (1965) they point to an association between the distribution of fox rabies and the occurrence of the type of caves where bats thrive. The most striking example is the Edwards plateau in Texas where fox rabies has persisted in the area of bat caves for over 30 years. In spite of these observations the exact link between the bats and foxes remains unknown.

Adamovich (1974) also notes discrete areas of rabies in the USSR. He believes that these are associated with erosion landscapes where mammalian vectors are less numerous and more mobile. Adamovich is unconvinced of any link between rabies foci and high fox (or other vector) densities. His density estimates, however, are based on figures from the pelt trade and snow tracking, both of which pose difficulties of interpretation.

Adamovich (1978) has gathered further data to support his hypothesis of topographically determined rabies foci ('natural territorial complexes'). By mapping rabies cases on topographic maps (scale 1:100 000) Adamovich concluded that foci of sylvatic rabies were not connected with the density of animals, but by the character of the locality which he believed determined the distribution of vectors and the

† A general theory of epidemiology (D. G. Kendall's pandemic threshold theorem) holds that epidemics can exceed a particular intensity only if the population density is greater than a particular threshold (Bailey 1975, p. 176). For example, if the average rabid fox infects less than one healthy fox before it dies then the disease dies out (exponentially), but if it contacts and infects more than one healthy fox then the disease begins to spread (exponentially). P. Bacon (personal communication) has restated Kendall's theorem in this context as: if the average 'distance searched' by a rabid fox is less than the average distance between susceptibles then the disease dies out, and vice versa. Bacon uses 'distance searched' as an area in effect, which is not analogous to nearest neighbour distances.

possibilities of contacts between them. Persistent foci occurred where polecats (*Mustela putorius*), racoon dogs (*Nyctereutes procyonoides*), and foxes overlapped. By detailed cartographic analysis of 933 domestic-animal rabies cases in the Bryansk region over 22 years (1954–75) and 195 cases in wild animals over 11 years, Adamovich calculated a co-efficient of epizooticity for each habitat. During the whole period 28 people died from rabies, 12 from infections from wildlife. Of all the wildlife cases the majority (38 per cent) were in ground broken by ravines, with fewer in other habitats: outwash plains (26 per cent), river valleys (20 per cent), loamy plains (16 per cent), and with none in moraine plains. From indices prepared from pelt numbers and snow tracking Adamovich believed the rugged ravine country to be ideal habitat for rabies vectors whose populations were in the proportion 1:4.6:6.9 for racoon dog:polecat:fox. From the incidence of rabies in these species examined in the laboratory he concluded that 24 per cent, 48 per cent, and 28 per cent of the wild populations respectively must be rabid. The incidence of cases in these three species had a differ-ent monthly pattern being greatest in January and May for foxes, March–April for racoon dogs and February and June for polecats when the latter accounted for 79 per cent and 68 per cent of all wildlife cases.

The polecate may play a role in passive storage of infection between epizootics, an idea which is supported by Gribanova *et al.*'s (1975) discovery of rabies-neutralizing antibodies in the blood of the Siberian polecate, *M. eversmanni* (see Chapter 6). Further, Adamovich believes that the racoon dog with latent storage of the rabies virus during hibernation can, on emergence from hibernation, critically tip the balance in starting fresh epizootics. The racoon dog's range has recently been expanding fast with habitat changes brought about by land recla-mation schemes and Adamovich notes that in places where rabies has long been endemic, but where racoon dogs have not yet arrived, epi-zootics have not broken out. He argues that fox densities have recently declined in his area, and elsewhere (Ukraine and Moldavia) but fox rabies has increased and hence that high fox densities are not a prerequisite for rabies epizootics.

I turn now to some of the attempts that have been made to curtail the spread of rabies epizootics among foxes. The possibility that reduction of fox populations could decelerate or even halt the spread of the disease has attracted health officials to proposals for reducing fox populations through intensive hunting of one sort or another. Fox populations are extremely resilient to control, not only because individuals are difficult to catch and kill, but more importantly because the reduced population has a considerable capacity for increasing again rapidly. This is evi-denced by the fact that the fox shows no sign of declining in numbers in

Britain despite the fact that in the region of 100 000 are killed annually (although it is not known what proportion of the population this represents). Despite the practical difficulties involved, governments throughout Europe and North America have sponsored large-scale attempts to reduce fox numbers in the hope of controlling rabies. The magnitude of some of these schemes is considerable. For example, in 1952 an attempt was made to stop the southerly spread of rabies through the province of Alberta. In this scheme 180 trappers were employed to work roughly 50 km of trapline each. Between them they were supplied with 6000 cyanide 'getters' and 429 000 strychnine cubes. During an 18-month period, the minimum kill was about 50 000 foxes, 35 000 coyotes, 4300 wolves, 7500 lynxes, 1850 bears, 500 skunks, 64 cougars, 1 wolverine, and 4 badgers. This scheme was supported by a back-up programme during which the farmers were supplied with 75 000 cyanide capsules and 163 000 strychnine cubes. It was estimated that the back-up programme itself accounted for between 60 000 and 80 000 coyotes. The ecological impact of such an enormous reduction during a relatively short period must have been considerable even for species which are relatively resilient. More lamentable still is that trapping and poisoning often have little specificity and in consequence individuals of non-target species, some of which may be rare, are also killed. Figure 5.11 emphasizes this point, showing how badgers were adversely affected by fox control schemes in Switzerland. A similar decline in badger numbers was seen in South Jutland after fox gassing in Denmark. T. Asferg (personal communication) has found in that region that before gassing one badger was shot for every ten foxes shot. Nowadays the ratio is one badger per eighty foxes, indicating how much more severely gassing affected badgers than it did foxes, the real target species (see also Asferg, Jepperson, and Sorensen (1977)).

The magnitude of the Alberta project is not without parallel. For example, an attempt to eradicate rabies in Mexico involved baiting an area of over 15 000 km² with cubes of horse meat containing sodium monofluoroacetate poison, which killed an estimated 18 000 wolves, coyotes, foxes, and skunks on the Mexican mainland, together with 10 000 more on the Baja California peninsula. Coyotes were supposedly exterminated over an area of nearly 13 000 km².

It is difficult to know how most appropriately to measure the cost of such schemes. One method might be in terms of lives saved were they successful, but there are depressingly few instances where the introduction of such control schemes can unequivocally be said to have resulted in the eradication of rabies. One exception to this may be the scheme in Denmark (see below). The cost in ecological disruption is another measure: the most straightforward aspect of this is that the removal of

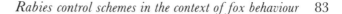

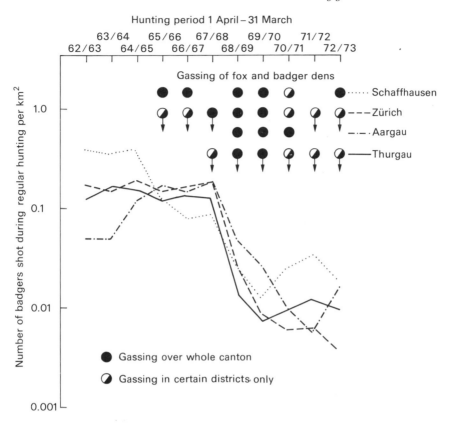

Fig. 5.11. The effect of gassing operations on the badger populations of four cantons in Switzerland. (After Wandeler *et al.* 1974*a*.)

predators frequently has a marked effect on populations of their prey.†
In Alberta, for example, the number of deer and moose increased greatly after the slaughter of carnivores which had previously preyed upon them; this resulted in serious over-grazing and consequent long-term damage to the range, which reduced its capacity to maintain big game herds. Perhaps the easiest direct costs can be measured financially

---

† In a recent paper, Mol (1977) suggests that in Poland the incidence of fox rabies depends on high densities of rodents and that such high densities are achieved in areas where avian predators are removed (p. 26).

in terms of the payments to trappers for wages, poisons, and traps; on one estimate the cost of each fox killed during a rabies reduction scheme in Tennessee was $208. The sums of money involved clearly are substantial and, as there are indications that current approaches do not fulfil the requirement of eradicating the disease, it would seem good business strategy to search for more efficient alternatives or even alternatives which are as efficient but less environmentally costly. Parks has suggested that post-epizootic trapping is ineffective and has little merit other than from the standpoint of public relations. If this view is correct, then perpetuation of the practice is morally untenable.

In Europe some attempt has been made to document the hunting pressure on fox populations. For instance, Lloyd *et al.* (1976) state that two foxes (of all ages) are removed per square kilometre from areas in Denmark, Switzerland, and the Federal Republic of Germany by hunters annually. They suggest that in rabies-free areas the removal rate lies between 1 and 1.4 foxes per km². Perhaps the most critical factor determining the plausibility of reducing fox numbers sufficiently to obliterate rabies is the proportion of vixens giving birth to cubs in earths that are suitable for gassing with hydrocyanic acid. Wandeler *et al.* (1974*c*) estimated that 45 per cent of litters in the Swabian Jura and 55 per cent in the Swiss Oberland were found outside earths. Even the most intensive gassing effort at earths would thus clearly fail to produce the 75 per cent reduction supposedly required to eradicate the disease and, indeed, as shown in Fig. 5.12, rabies has continued to exist in the Swabian Jura in spite of intensive gassing. Wandeler and his colleagues also point out that the gassing operation itself ultimately becomes self-defeating because the proportion of available earths gradually dwindles as they are gassed, with the possible result that vixens increasingly select cubbing sites above ground. Indeed, should the gassing continue, one could imagine that natural selection will ultimately favour vixens which give birth above ground. Wandeler's point is made amply by his discovery in Switzerland that the proportion of litters found in earths decreased from 63 per cent to 49 per cent after a single year of gassing (see below). However Toma and Andral (1977) have suggested that gassing earths throughout a belt at least 80 km wide in advance of the epizootic front may hinder its progress. The extent to which foxes' denning habits vary from one region to the next is illustrated by Lloyd's (personal communication) estimate that in mid-Wales 1 earth in 120 is occupied during the spring, whereas in Pembrokeshire 1 in 11 is utilized.

Is there any evidence of the effect of such control measures on the behaviour of individual foxes which would enable us to understand better the processes being effected? Sadly, the answer is that there is very

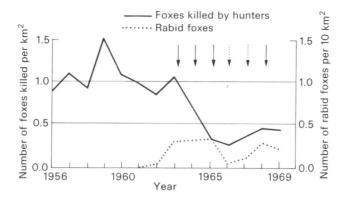

Fig. 5.12. Changes in the fox population density index in the Swabian Jura area (7191 km²) of Baden-Württemberg, West Germany, from 1956 to 1969. Solid arrows indicate gassing campaigns; broken ones indicate incomplete gassing operations. (After Wandeler *et al.* 1974c.)

little evidence on this point, although one case-history, followed by Sargeant (1972) will be mentioned further below. However, there is a general biological phenomenon which may be very relevant: the 'vacuum effect'.

The principle underlying the vacuum effect harkens back to the concepts involved with territoriality which were explained above. Territorial behaviour, while ostensibly directed towards defending an area of ground, is indirectly an adaptation towards securing the resources available within that area of ground. By defending a territory an animal may in effect be defending its food supply for the future. The finite quantity of resources available is often insufficient for all members of the population, so part of the community become territory holders while the remainder form a reservoir referred to as 'surplus'. Under these circumstances, when a territory becomes vacant because of the death or emigration of its tenant, the space can be filled by surplus individuals whose survival depends on finding a territory. The idea of the biological vacuum is that a vacant territory rapidly sucks up an animal from the reservoir and so is soon filled again. This phenomenon certainly happens with many animals and bedevils control schemes that attempt to reduce the numbers of territorial individuals: no sooner has a territory been vacated than it is occupied by a newcomer. Since it is possible in animal populations for the reservoir actually to constitute the majority of individuals, at least during some seasons, the supply of newcomers may be effectively inexhaustible. If such an effect operates in fox populations it would be relevant to our design of control schemes which involve killing foxes, since the reduction of the population in one locality might simply precipitate an influx of animals from a neighbouring area. To minimize such a risk, Toma and Andral (1977) have suggested that gassing and other control operations should be conducted on as large a scale as possible. It is quite likely that the vacuum operates only after piecemeal removal of foxes and hence does not apply to massive anti-rabies schemes, which are nevertheless beset with many inadequacies.

An example, albeit from a very different species, illustrates this vacuum phenomenon. Great tits, *Parus major*, like foxes in some regions, are territorial and live in pairs which defend their patch against intruders. Their behaviour has been studied intensively by John Krebs, who has constructed maps depicting the exact territory boundaries of eight pairs of great tits in a woodland near Oxford. Krebs (1977) also tape recorded the individual calls of the birds occupying each of these territories. During one morning in February he captured and removed all these resident birds from their territories. In some territories (called experimental) he replaced the birds with a loudspeaker which played the recorded songs of the original inmate of that territory. In other territories (called controls) the speakers played some irrelevant noise at the same intervals in which real song was being played in the experimental territories. Within two days Krebs found that all the vacant territories had been refilled and eight new pairs of great tits were in residence. He also discovered that the control territories were filled much quicker than the experimental ones and thus demonstrated the role of song in proclaiming territory ownership. Krebs demonstrated that the new birds had come from two sources, both of which might be bracketed under the umbrella of 'surplus': some came from neighbouring hedgerows where they had maintained territories but where the habitat was less appropriate for the bird; others came from an itinerant population of great tits that drift through the wood passing through occupied territories in a way reminiscent of the itinerant foxes described above.

There are few data on this phenomenon in mammals, largely because they are so difficult to study. However, one might expect similar forces to operate on populations of predatory birds and mammals. Newton *et al.* (1977) have shown that in 17 species of birds of prey (from 9 genera) there was rapid replacement of removed territory holders. In one case eight female lesser kestrels arrived in turn to take up residence in a territory as their predecessors were removed. For the European kestrel Newton (personal communication) tells me of six cases where a captured territory holder was replaced within an hour of its removal!

Do foxes respond to vacated territories in the same way as great tits, kestrels, and others and if so, do they do so with the same speed? Two authorities on fox behaviour, Lloyd (Wales) and Jensen (Denmark), have doubts about the speed with which foxes recolonize cleared areas. Lloyd points out that after a massive fox control programme in an area of Pembrokeshire there was a back-up programme the following year. During the back-up programme the number of foxes killed was minimal compared to the cull during the first year. Lloyd argues that this suggests that any vacuum that exists was working very slowly. However, there are alternative explanations. For instance, Lloyd's Pembrokeshire study area has a relatively high fox population density occupying what appears to be a rich and varied habitat. Such conditions have been shown to be favourable for the establishment of fox groups including more than one vixen (Macdonald 1977*a*). Even the most optimistic hunters would admit the difficulty of killing more than about 70 per cent of foxes in an area, and it seems likely that after the initial year of fox reduction in Pembrokeshire many family groups retained at least one adult member. Since the available evidence suggests that the only way for a female to become a member of such a group and to gain occupancy of the group territory is to be born into it, any such animals might themselves repel intruders with the result that the population density could only increase in these territories as another generation of cubs was born. I have seen foxes of both sexes attacking intruders of either sex, and so if one member of a pair or group is killed it is possible that the remaining member might repel intruders, even of the other sex, until the next breeding season. The relations between foxes of each sex with their neighbours needs much more study (see also Preston 1973). There are few data on the life-histories of foxes subjected to experimental control schemes to evaluate these various explanations, or for that matter, the dozens of other possibilities. The way in which foxes colonize and explore unoccupied habitats certainly requires considerable study. One interesting example comes from Anglesey, where they were introduced in 1962. Local reports suggest that as the fox population grew it remained concentrated in one area for at least the next decade.

An interesting case where an unoccupied territory was not immediately taken by an itinerant animal has been described. Sargeant (1972) conducted a detailed study on radio-tracked foxes, particularly in relation to the effect of these predators on wildfowl populations. In one case he had defined the boundaries of several neighbouring fox territories when one dog fox and his six cubs were killed. The fate of the mother of these cubs was unknown because she was not radio-tagged, but the dog and vixen from the adjacent territory at once expanded their home range to incorporate that which had previously been occupied by the deceased dog fox. Sargeant speculates that the previous vixen had either been killed or had left the area. Sargeant tells me that this new expanded home range, nearly double the size of the original, was maintained for at least the following year. Such expansion in the event of neighbouring deaths could also account for Lloyd's observation that his study population remained at a low level even a year after intensive slaughter.

An animal attempting to defend a territory twice as large as that which had previously supported it is in a position not dissimilar to a businessman who considers taking over one of his competitors: the potential profits may be increased but the cost of running the business increases too. In the latter case, the cost may be money, while in the first it is the energy expended in repelling intruders, but the principles are similar: if the costs of defence outweigh the benefits of, for example, additional food, then the territory will contract until it is economically defensible. This, in simple terms, is probably how territory sizes are geared to food supply. Thus, over time and under sufficient attack by itinerant animals, it would be costly for a fox to maintain a territory twice as big as that which could support it unless, of course, it was able to increase its group size and hence enlist co-operation in defence. For this reason one might expect that territories would contain roughly the same quantity of critical resources, like food, and hence the territories in the same habitat would be of approximately the same size. That this principle holds for tawny owls has been neatly demonstrated by Hirons (1977), who has shown that each owl's territory, irrespective of its overall size, contains roughly the same length of hedgerow, the critical habitat required for catching rodents.

The effects of fox-reduction schemes conducted in the name of rabies control will be properly understood and open to judgement only when the relationship between habitat quality, territory and group size, and the economics of defence are fully unravelled. One measurable aspect of the inadequacies of fox-reduction schemes is the species' rapid rate of repopulation. This has received considerable attention from Bögel, Arata, Moegle, and Knorpp (1974). These authors measured fox population density indirectly through the 'hunting indicator of population density' (HIPD) in areas of Europe where the springtime populations were estimated at 0.9–1.2 adult foxes/km², in the absence of rabies. They believe that hunting statistics, when collected from areas measuring over 2000 km², provide a useful measure of the apparent change in fox population density within defined areas. This must normally require averaging over widely different habitats.

The HIPD in Switzerland showed an apparent crash in fox numbers of 50–60 per cent when rabies struck. In North Baden in West

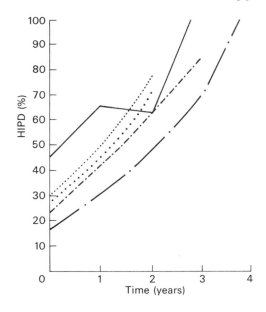

Fig. 5.13. The recovery of the HIPD index of fox population density (see text) year by year following the passage of rabies and the cessation of gassing operations. Each line represents a different area of Baden-Württemberg, West Germany. (From Bögel *et al.* 1974.)

Germany, rabies together with intensified hunting between 1957–63 brought fox bags to about 40 per cent of their original levels. Bögel *et al.* measured the rate at which fox populations recovered in different areas after the epizooty had passed and intensive gassing stopped. This is shown for six areas in Fig. 5.13. The HIPD recovered from 20–30 per cent of its original level in about 4 years, and the maximum increase of HIPD was 71 per cent. Using these observations as a starting-point, Bögel *et al.* attempted to derive a reliable relationship between the rate of population recovery and the extent of previous decimation such that they could reliably predict how long it would take for a decimated population to return to its pre-epizootic numbers. They computed the †

† The formula used assumes exponential increase rather than a probably more realistic asymptotic one. Bögel *et al.* calculate the percentage increase over a preceding year as equal to

   100 [(*Final population/Reduced population*) to the power of 1/*Recovery period* − 1].

Thus, if a population is reduced by 80 per cent and the HIPD takes 4 years to recover, then the population recovers at an annual rate of increase of 49.5 per cent, since

   $100 [(100/20)^{1/4} − 1] = 100 (1.495 − 1) = 49.5$ per cent.

For a full explanation see Bögel *et al.* (1974).

percentage increase of the HIPD over the figure for the preceding year and so derived recovery curves.

The mean rate of annual increase obscures the rapid initial recovery and the levelling off as the population nears its previous level. The authors' best estimate for the real pattern of recovery is shown in Fig. 5.14 which allows predictions to be made concerning the speed of recovery of populations reduced to different extents and monitored by HIPD. The authors believe that a knowledge of the rate of recovery is crucial to authorities planning fox reduction as a means of stemming a rabies epizooty and believe that the estimates yielded by Fig. 5.14 provide a ready means of predicting this information. It would be interesting to know what biological processes underlie these curves. How ever the HIPD should be interpreted, where it falls below 0.3 fox/km² there has never been a positive incidence of rabies. Further-more the velocity of the rabies front seems to be quite independent of the hunting indicator. Incidentally, Braunschweig (1980) provides another model for estimating fox population density. He concludes that hunting

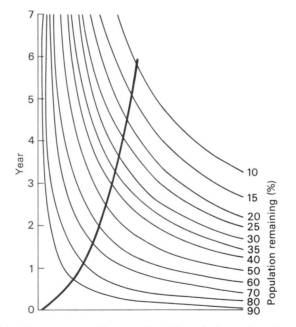

Fig. 5.14. This diagram provides a rule of thumb for estimating the speed of recovery of fox populations after they have been decimated by rabies. The intersection of the bold line with the other lines indicates the number of years required for the population to recover, depending on the proportion which escaped the passage of the disease. (From Bögel *et al.* 1974.)

mortality does not play an important role in regulating fox numbers and, further, that only 2 per cent of all rabid foxes are ever found.

Some indication that foxes fill up gaps created by the removal of territory holders comes from figures gathered on the distances over which juveniles disperse in habitats where rabies has decimated the population. L. Andral (personal communication) reports that juvenile foxes normally disperse over 20–40 km, but that behind the epizootic front the distance is considerably less.

One effect of fox-reduction schemes that is partially understood is the influence of hunting† pressure on the age-structure of the population. The age-structure, in turn, may have profound consequences on social organization and community structure. The most obvious effect of hunting pressure seems to be an alteration of the proportion of the population which is young. This phenomenon was first pointed out in 1967 by Knowlton, who was working on coyotes in south-west Texas. He noted that of coyotes killed in an intensively controlled study area, there were 15.7 young animals for every adult, whereas in an area with only light control, the ratio was 4 young per adult. Indications that a similar effect on age structure operated in fox populations was apparent from Phillips's study in central Iowa. He collected dead foxes from a zone where intensive hunting had operated for several years under the influence of a double bounty scheme. Phillips found 5.6 juveniles for every adult in the population. In South Jutland (Denmark) Jensen and Nielsen found 3.02 cubs per adult in the area where a bounty scheme had also been used in an attempt to reduce fox populations. In contrast, working with a tiny sample relative to these previous studies, I have found a young-to-old ratio of 0.26:1 in a completely undisturbed habitat.

The ages of foxes can be assessed from growth-rings in their teeth. (An annual ring is laid down in a way reminiscent of the ageing process of trees.) Using this method it has been possible in various studies to discover the percentage of the population in each age class. A summary of four studies (Table 5.4) shows that in areas of the most intensive control the proportion of juvenile and one-year-old animals to adults is relatively greater. Of course, the sample size of dead animals examined in my own study area is tiny compared to the other studies (because there was no hunting pressure on the foxes), but in spite of this there are clear differences. What effects on the social organization of foxes can this alteration in age structure have when it is induced by hunting pressure? The answer may lie in the altered young-to-adult ratio mentioned

---

† Hunting is here taken to be the combined methods of fox control, and not traditional hunting with hounds in the strictly British sense.

Table 5.4   Proportion between animals younger than one year (juv.) and older than 1½ years (ad.) in winter (between 1 September and 31 March) compared between samples with different causes of death.

	Regular shooting (rabies-free area)	Regular shooting (rabies-endemic area)	Trapping (rabies-endemic area)	Road kill	Sarcoptic mange	Other diseases	Rabid foxes
Number of animals	821	594	166	182	81	271	992
Juv. (%)	65	71	67	77	51	62	45
Ad. (%)	35	29	33	23	49	38	55

Rabies-positive foxes are on the average significantly older than negative foxes from the same area. In all other sampling categories juveniles prevail with no difference between rabies-endemic and rabies-free areas.
Source: Wandeler *et al.* 1974*c* (and see Wandeler 1976*b*, Table 3).

above. In this context, the study of Hewson and Kolb (1973) is particularly interesting: these biologists from the Department of Agriculture for Scotland investigated the fate of foxes killed in Scotland between 1948 and 1970. Large numbers are killed each year either by the Forestry Commission or by fox clubs (consortia of local farmers who organize their own bounty schemes); between 1965 and 1966 more than 10 000 foxes were killed.

The researchers discovered that in general the number of adult foxes killed each year by the Forestry Commission between 1962 and 1970 had increased (Fig. 5.15(a)). During the same years, however, with increasing fox numbers, they found that the cub-to-adult ratio was decreasing (Fig. 5.15(b)); that is, while the number of adults killed each year has generally been increasing in different areas of Scotland, the number of cubs has remained relatively constant from year to year. These findings led Hewson and Kolb to propose that density-dependent factors were affecting the reproductive success of the population. I suggested earlier that some sort of density-dependent effect explained Jan Englund's data on the proportion of barren vixens in his Swedish populations and that observations on the behaviour of individual foxes within family groups had shown that in larger groups social factors are exerted to repress the reproduction of subordinate vixens. It may be, then, that in the parts of Scotland from which Hewson and Kolb's sample was drawn, the fox population has reached its upper limit of density so that social factors are limiting the number of cubs born into

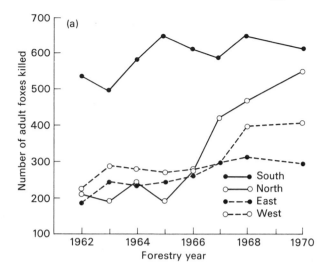

Fig. 5.15(a). The number of foxes killed each year by the Forestry Commission in Scotland from 1962 to 1970 in each of four Conservancies. (Until 1968 the Forestry year was from 1 October to 30 September; it was then changed to 1 April–31 March. Data for the 18-month gap have been excluded.) (After Hewson and Kolb 1973.)

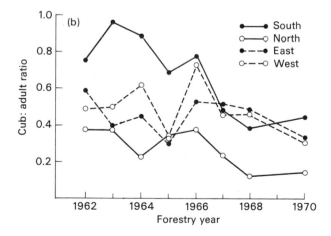

Fig. 5.15(b). The cub: adult ratios for foxes killed by the Forestry Commission in each of four Conservancies from 1962 to 1970. (After Hewson and Kolb 1973.)

the population each year. Such social factors may not operate in the populations that are heavily controlled, such as that studied by Phillips in Iowa, where there may be too few adult foxes to colonize the available habitat and so enough room for each adult vixen to maintain a territory and to breed, thus increasing the productivity per vixen and the juvenile-to-adult ratio. In addition, Trautman, Fredrickson, and Carter (1974) believe that litter sizes increase in heavily controlled populations. They found that the overall average litter size over 6 years of control was 63 per cent larger (from 4.7 to 7.67) than before control began, although the initial figure is based only on one year.

Whether it is desirable in terms of epizootiology to have a stable, self-regulating fox population or an unstable, growing and 'bottom heavy' one, is unknown. However, all else being equal (which it is not), one might argue that a high proportion of juveniles might lead to a relatively mobile population as they dispersed, which could accelerate the spread of the disease.

The various European authorities involved in attempted rabies control through fox reduction campaigns have published accounts of their work, much of which was summarized by Wandeler and his colleagues (Wandeler *et al.* 1974*a*, *b*, *c*,). Table 5.5 summarizes their data on the incidence of the disease in wild and domestic animals for the German *land* of Hessen, for Denmark, and for Switzerland. As mentioned above, the fox plays a central role and cases among other wild species such as stone-martens, badgers, and roe deer disappear at much the same time, or soon after the disappearance of fox rabies from an area. Wandeler and his colleagues state that the incidence of rabies was very clearly dependent on the density of foxes. In three Swiss cantons, shown in Fig. 5.16, they have followed the effects of gassing earths and of rabies on the number of foxes killed by hunters; the combined effect is a reduction of hunting yield to about 20 per cent of its previous level. The incidence of rabies cases reported in these cantons dropped very rapidly as the epizooty spread suggesting that the risk of infection was lowered much faster than the risk of being killed by a hunter as the fox population density fell (Fig. 5.16). Thus the disease rapidly changed from accounting for from 30–60 per cent of the foxes reported dead each year to an almost undetectable level of less than one rabid fox in roughly 200 km^2 during the time when hunting figures fell only by about 20 per cent. From these data Wandeler *et al.* (1974*a*) conclude:

'This relationship between fox density and rabies clearly shows that fox rabies in the front wave of the epizootic is not merely an indicator of a virus reservoir in another unknown animal species, but that the epidemic depends on fox-to-fox spread' (p. 747).

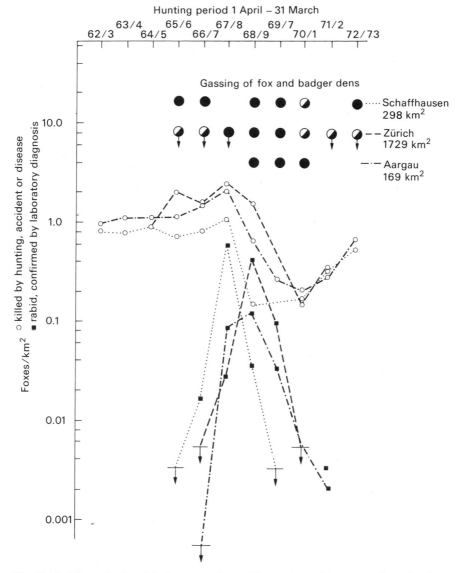

Fig. 5.16. The relationship between fox rabies and the fox population density index derived from hunting records in the Swiss cantons of Zürich, Schaffhausen, and Aagau. (After Wandeler *et al.* 1974*a*.)

Comparing areas of different fox densities, it seems that the efficacy of fox reduction schemes may be very different. For example, in the high density areas the disease itself, perhaps in combination with gassing, may depress the population so low that the epizooty terminates. Where

Table 5.5   Distribution of rabies among wild and domestic animals

Species	Hessen 1953–71† Rabid animals		Denmark 1964–5 & 1969–70 Rabid animals		Switzerland 1.3.67–31.3.73			
					Rabies-free area	Rabies-endemic area		
							Positive animals	
	Number	%	Number	%	Negative animals	Negative animals	Number	% of rabid animals
Wild animals								
Red fox	5481	58.49	186	79	2864	2048	2147	83
Badger	87	0.93	—	—	166	222	100	4.0
Stone-marten			7	3.0	283	481	63	2.5
Pine-marten			—	—	12	22	1	0.04
Stoat	145	1.55	—	—	17	31	0	0
Weasel			—	—	—	—	—	—
Polecat			—	—	10	44	5	0.2
Roe-deer	1399	14.93	6	2.5	213	727	129	5.0
Red Deer			—	—	3	34	1	0.04
Chamois			—	—	7	25	5	0.2
Wild Boar			—	—	9	2	0	0
Hare			—	—	55	166	0	0
Squirrel	76‡	0.81	—	—	71	163	0	0
Other Rodent			—	—	87	154	1§	0.04
Bats			—	—	11	7	0	0
Insectivors			—	—	20	52	0	0
Birds			—	—	14	20	0	0
Total Wildlife	7188	76.71%	199	84.5%			2452	95 %
Domestic animals					Switzerland Total examined	Rabies-positive		
Dogs	495	5.29	1	0.4	346		11	0.4
Domestic cats	923	9.84	12	5.1	1740		50	1.9
Cattle	594	6.34	14	6.0	100		40	1.6
Sheep			9	3.8	168		19	0.7
Goats			—	—	12		3	0.1
Swine			1	0.4	4		0	0
Horse	171¶	1.82	1	0.4	5		1	0.04
Donkey			—	—	2		1	0.04
Other domestic animals			—	—	14		0	0
Total Domestic animals	2184	23.29%	38	16.1%			125	5 %

† Routine diagnostic material, not collected in view of epidemiological evaluation.
‡ Total of all wildlife species examined in Hessen, other than the 8 species above.
§ One mouse salivary gland (from *Apodemus flavicollis*) positive in the 3rd mouse passage.
¶ Total of all domestic animals examined in Hessen, other than dogs, cats, and cattle.
Source: Wandeler *et al.* 1974*a*.

fox densities are lower, Wandeler *et al* speculate that the disease does not sufficiently reduce the population to curb the epizooty. In these zones of intermediate fox densities (e.g. Swiss Cantons St. Gallen and Appenzell) they believe particularly rigorous hunting effort is required.

In the course of examining foxes for signs of rabies Wandeler also discovered the age of the animals. He found that both within and outside rabies endemic areas yearlings comprised the majority of healthy foxes. In contrast the majority of rabid foxes are older than 1½ years old (Table 5.4). The proportions of young to old animals in rabid and healthy populations throughout the year are shown in Fig. 5.17. It is hard to resolve the extent to which these figures reflect greater susceptibility of older foxes to rabies rather than of younger foxes to other methods of hunting. In fact, Jan Englund (1970) has already shown that juveniles are more susceptible to hunters than are old foxes.

Using these basic data Wandeler *et al.* (1974c) went on to consider the ecology and biology of the fox in relation to control operations. In particular they were concerned to estimate the fox population density in their study area. They believe that in their study areas all healthy vixens give birth to cubs (although this is not true for all habitats as discussed above) with an average litter size of 4.67 and a sex ratio of males to females of 1.2:1.0. Using reports of the location of fox-breeding earths they employed these statistics to compute the fox population density. They assumed that the population was stable, i.e. that annual productivity equals annual losses. For the cantons Jura, Mittelland, and Oberland these estimates are shown in Table 5.6, which shows that the computed population density of adults prior to cubbing varied between 0.35–0.56 foxes per km². As stated above, fox density varies far outside these limits in different habitats. Without mortality, a fox population in which every vixen bred annually at this rate would treble each year, which explains the resilience of foxes to even the most intense control.

Table 5.6   Calculation of population density at its annual peak in summer

Region	Observed litters/km²	Observed cubs/litter	Calculated annual productivity (foxes/km²)	Foxes registered killed and found dead per km²	Population density (foxes/km²) Before whelping	After whelping
Jura	0.24		1.12	1.13	0.53	1.65
Mittelland	0.21	4.67	0.98	0.95	0.46	1.44
Oberland	0.16		0.75	0.78	0.35	1.10

Source: Wandeler *et al.* (1974c)

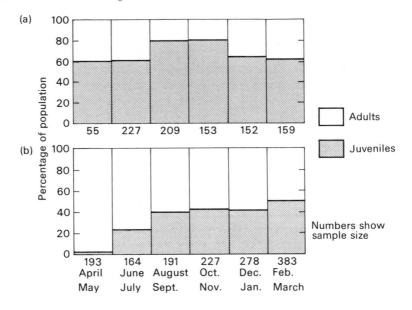

Fig. 5.17. The proportions of young to old foxes (a) in healthy populations and (b) in rabid fox populations in Switzerland. (After Wandeler *et al.* 1974*b*.)

At the time of publishing their results Wandeler *et al.* believed that the combined effects of rabies, hunting, and gassing were sufficient to reduce fox populations to a level at which the disease died out. However, they argue that such reduction can be achieved only with rabies and gassing acting in concert. For this reason they raised doubts as to the long-term efficacy of such control schemes, since there is some evidence that in repeatedly gassed zones the foxes begin to breed away from earths. For example, in one zone gassed in 1969 they found that 63 per cent ($n = 404$) of litters were in earths; the next year only 49 per cent of 201 litters were in natural (ungassable) caves had risen correspondingly.

Some of the same data on European rabies have been reanalysed by Sayers, Mansourian, Phan Tin, and Bögel (1977), who have studied the pattern of wildlife rabies epizooty in a 133 km × 133 km area in Baden-Württemberg, West Germany. Their study entailed sophisticated analyses based on statistical communication theory and endeavoured to tackle two questions: first to elucidate any relationship between the pattern of rabies cases and physical features of their study area and second, to find some way of defining the 'wave-front' of the epizooty that was sufficiently robust to be predictively useful. Taking all the cases reported between 1963 and 1970 Sayers and his colleagues drew rabies 'contour' maps which illustrated the spatial distribution of cases. Essentially these maps correspond with physical features such as upland terrain and rivers which impeded the progress of the disease. Next, the authors further split the data into epochs of 4 months so that temporal characteristics of the distribution of infected foxes could be followed in detail. The results are pictured in Fig. 5.18, from which it is clear that having invaded the study area in 1963 the epizooty finally left from the south-west during 1968–70. During that time the axis of the epizooty altered between south-east and south. Sayers *et al.* point to indications of several separate progressive foci together with regions of recurrent outbreaks where the pattern appeared different to that during the original epizooty. The authors were particularly attracted to the idea of analysing both the global features of the entire epizooty and then, independently, the foci of groups of cases. In considering the entire epizooty they discovered that one variable, namely the distribution of uplands, accounted for 14 per cent of the variance in the pattern of case-occurrence.

Turning to the problem of defining the position of the wave-front, and using this definition in the hope of predicting the position of further cases, Sayers *et al.* used a statistical procedure called the expectation density function. This involves a complex analysis of the juxtaposition of all known cases to assess how likely it is when considering a known case that another case will occur at various near-by locations. The procedure is carried out for each case in turn so that ultimately the likelihood of neighbouring cases occurring in various positions relative to every other case can be assessed and the entire pattern broken down into a series of wave-fronts which link cases whose relative positions share the same probability. The alternative to this procedure would simply be to link peripheral case occurrences to describe the epizooty front, irrespective of the statistical features of their juxtaposition. Using Sayers's more subtle method Fig. 5.18 shows that after 1966 the wave-front altered from a south-south-easterly orientation to a southern or south-south-westerly one. Further, periods of rapid progress are discernible. In fact the main change in direction coincided with the leading edge of the wave reaching the Danube. Subsequently, Sayers *et al.* analysed the pattern of occurrence of rabid foxes to reveal temporary foci of infection whose trajectory could also be traced in part to physical features such as the Danube river or Jura mountains. While radio-tracking itinerant dog foxes I have frequently found their movements to be influenced by rivers. Storm *et al.* (1976) also recorded the effect of both rivers and towns on fox movements. In fact, even the borders of resident fox

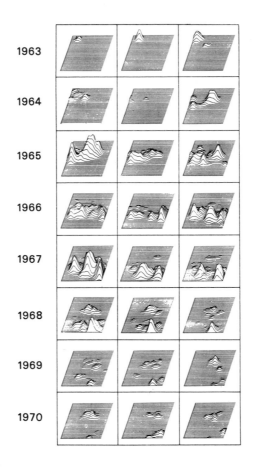

Fig. 5.18. Smoothed interpolated plots of the occurrence of rabies by 4-monthly periods in a part of Baden-Württemberg, West Germany, 1963–70. (Figure courtesy of B. McA. Sayers.)

territories often correspond to topographical features such as roads or field boundaries.

M. Thai Thien Nghia (1977) has conducted analyses similar to those of Sayers *et al.* (1977), again finding that the main spatial shift of the disease occurs in winter. He also found some additional paths of high-velocity spread and discovered a close correspondence between these and the network of main roads in the area which led him to the following conclusions:

1. Roads seem to be the main medium of fast rabies propagation.
2. Rural areas, and in particular national parks are ideal for such propagation. On the contrary urban zones do not particularly favour it.
3. Slow propagation areas correspond to areas where main roads are non-existent.
4. Motorways (M11 linking Karlsruhe–Stuttgard–München in the north and M31 between Rottweil and Singen in the south) seem abruptly to stop the rabies progression. Lake Bodensee is another cause of such a halt.
5. Crossings of the Danube River generally slow down rabies progress.

The significance of roads in my own study areas seem to be threefold, and ties up with Thai Thien Nghia's model. Roads are both travel routes and often territory borders (the two aspects may be linked), and motorways seem to discourage fox movements. Of course roads themselves may be routed in particular habitats, e.g. through valleys, and hence association between fox movements and roads may be a secondary effect. Using quite different methods Steck (1975) reported rather similar relationships between geographical features and rabies' progress. He found that self-limiting epizootics occurred in small alpine valleys. The mountain ridges reach 2000 m above sea-level and presumably limit the movement of fox communities locked within.

Before leaving fox-reduction schemes we should consider the one which appears to have been most successful, namely that in South Jutland. The Danes began to kill foxes with the idea of halting the spread of rabies when, in 1953, the disease was approaching them through Germany. By 1964 rabies had crossed Danish borders. In the years that followed the epizootic spread northwards, and the zones within which foxes were killed by gassing and poisoning with strychnine nitrate were gradually increased (Fig. 5.19). The idea was to form a belt where foxes were heavily controlled that stretched across the whole of Southern Jutland and reached 20 kilometres north of the epizootic front. In the adjoining 20-kilometre zone a slightly less intensive campaign was continued and a bounty paid for foxes and badgers. The vaccination of dogs was made compulsory and dogs found away from buildings were shot. This scheme was apparently successful, perhaps because the neck

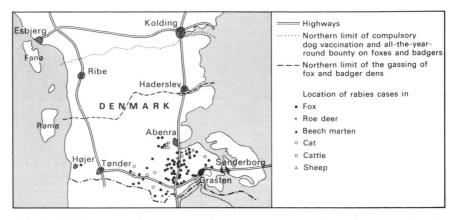

Fig. 5.19. The campaign against rabies in Southern Jutland, Denmark, during 1964–5. The limits of vaccination and gassing operations are shown together with the locations of individual outbreaks of the disease. (After Müller 1969.)

of land through which the disease had to spread was sufficiently narrow for an intensive effort to make a substantial reduction in the fox population. However, as soon as the intensity of the control scheme was relaxed, a second outbreak occurred. This too was stopped and once more control was relaxed until in 1977 a further case, heralding a third wave which has not yet been halted (WHO 1979).

Müller and Nielson (1972) point out that the 1969–70 and 1964–5 outbreaks occurred in different parts of South Jutland and that there is no evidence to suggest that the second epizooty had its origins in a hidden focus surviving from the original outbreak. They conclude that both originated from rabid foxes crossing from Schleswig-Holstein. Müller (1969, 1971) has documented the course of both these epizooties in great detail; during the first outbreak the 83 cases were distributed amongst 63 foxes, 4 roe deer, 1 stone marten, 7 cats, 5 cattle, and 3 sheep. Jensen too sampled hunting records for foxes during 1967 and found that within the gassing zone the returns were 0.2 fox/100 ha as opposed to the normal 1 fox/100 ha. Further north where there was intensified shooting, but no gassing in response to the epizooty the bag fell from 1.0–1.5 foxes/100 ha to 1.0 fox/100 ha. Müller concluded that bounty shooting alone can reduce fox populations by 25 per cent, and shooting and gassing can produce an 80 per cent reduction. Similar results were obtained during the 1969–70 outbreak when 155 cases were reported. Müller notes that as soon as the disease gained a foothold north of the old gassing zone it spread quickly through a new area (the two areas in 1969 had bag records of 0.15 and 1.0 fox per 100 ha

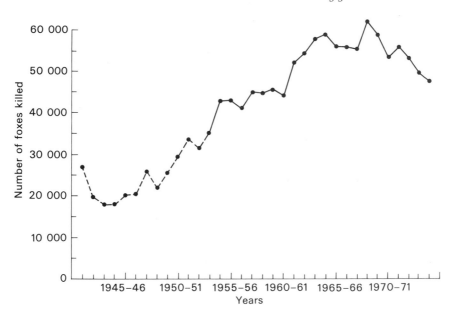

Fig. 5.20. The number of foxes killed in Denmark from 1941/2 to 1974/5 according to the Danish bag record. Until and including 1953/4 the bag was not corrected for unsurrendered licences. (After Jensen 1977.)

respectively). On two occasions during this spread an isolated case of fox rabies appeared 25-30 km ahead of the main outbreak.

Jensen (1970) reported some interesting consequences of the anti-fox measures taken as a consequence of rabies in Denmark. He found that in an area where the number of foxes killed annually fell from 5000 in 1964 to 2000 in 1968 the bag of hare, partridge, and pheasant all increased by 50–100 per cent. Spittler (1973) has presented similar data for Nordrhein-Westfalen and Trautman *et al.* (1974) record more than a doubling of jack rabbit numbers after intensive fox-control operations.†　Irrespective of the effect of rabies on Danish bag records it is interesting to note that the annual toll had been gradually increasing since 1945 (Jensen 1977) from around 20 000 to over 60 000 foxes per year (Fig. 5.20). Whether this build-up in fox population to a peak in the 1960s has any bearing on the outbreak of rabies during that period is unknown. Indeed, the ecological forces underlying the increase in foxes killed is unknown. The annual bag should be considered in the light of Jensen's estimate that there are 23 703 registered hunters in Denmark.

† Other accounts of the impact of foxes on game species can be found in Johnson and Sargeant (1977) and Pils and Martin (1978).

The extent to which the Danish rabies-control programme is a success story is cast in some doubt since the disease also disappeared from Schleswig-Holstein during the same period in the absence of any attempts at control. The intensity of these Danish control schemes was such that it was impractical to maintain them over anything but a short period. Nevertheless, the very detailed documentation of rabies progress in Denmark makes it a specially interesting case for further study. For instance, one important operation for rabies modelling is the distance travelled by rabid foxes. Two cases from Denmark suggest that foxes had travelled about 16 km, but the general consensus seems to be that few go further than 8 km.

Clues to the behaviour of 40 rabid foxes come from Johnston and Hroncock (1970) who studied their stomach contents. Apart from conventional prey items they found remains of other species, for example 3 per cent contained racoon, 3 per cent porcupine, 5 per cent each of striped skunk dog, and 25 per cent fox. Fifteen per cent of these foxes smelled strongly of skunk, indicating an encounter while both participants were alive and 13 per cent had eaten a small portion of fox such as a few whiskers or an ear. The authors speculate that these were torn from living victims (one wonders whether other foxes are found missing these components). Fox flesh (and carnivore flesh in general) is low among fox food preferences (Macdonald 1977b). One quarter of the stomachs contained faeces (I have seen healthy foxes eating herbivore dung), 17 per cent had eaten fox faeces, and snow tracking revealed that rabid foxes also ate snow on which other foxes had urine-marked, which is abnormal (see Macdonald 1979b).

Clearly the efficacy of fox reduction schemes in stemming the tide of rabies, far less eradicating the disease, is in some doubt. Møllgaard (personal communication) believes, on the basis of statistics gathered in Denmark, that an effective gassing campaign can reduce a fox population by up to 70–5 per cent. The greatest problem is our lack of understanding of the effects of such assassination campaigns on fox behaviour. In spite of the effort which has gone into modelling rabies epizootics, we are still unable to answer relatively simple questions. How, for example, does reducing the fox population to a quarter of its previous level affect the number of new animals infected by each victim? Does it result in a fourfold decrease or do the foxes somehow change their behaviour so that the incidence of the disease does not decline linearly with a reduction in fox numbers? If the latter is the case, how would the reproduction rate be affected by, say, a 50 per cent vaccination scheme as opposed to an 80 per cent kill? Before models can be expected to answer practical questions of this sort much more basic field information is needed on the fox's natural history.

6 Some other wild vectors

In Europe the fox is the main wildlife vector of rabies, although many other species of mammal are also involved. Elsewhere other species play a key role: in Asia, jackals, bandicoots, mongooses, and bats are all involved, while in Africa, genets, Cape foxes, bat-eared foxes, honey badgers, mongooses, and ground squirrels have been implicated. The epizootiology of rabies is relatively simple in Europe, where only one species is apparently important. Over much of the Americas there are several different vector species and the epizootiological picture is greatly complicated by this. A few of the Caribbean islands are exceptional in that one species of mongoose is the principal wildlife host.

Rabies in Grenada is especially interesting. It has been continuously under surveillance for ten years (Everard *et al.*, personal communication). Since 1968 there has been only one human death, together with nearly 700 recorded animal cases. Everard and his colleagues report that the mongoose, *Herpestes auropunctatus*, is the main vector. In addition rabies was confirmed in an insectivorous bat (*Molossus major*) which bit a woman in 1961; in 1974 Price and Everard (1977) reported isolating rabies from a frugivorous bat (*Artibeus jamaicensis*) and the presence of rabies-serum neutralizing antibodies (SNA) in several other species of bats. Nevertheless, 57.2 per cent of human post-exposure treatments arise directly from mongoose bites and 1.3 per cent of the 12 000 mongooses trapped between 1968 and 1977 were diagnosed rabid.

Everard, Baer, and James (1974) have described the history of rabies on Grenada. The island measures about 350 km² with a human population of over 95 000. In the decade prior to 1972, 4.05 per 100 000 people died of rabies, which compares with 0.007 36 in the USA. The first attempt to control rabies on Grenada was made in 1955 when, in addition to vaccinating dogs, 20 000 baits contained thallium sulphate were distributed over 200 km². An estimated 10 000 mongooses succumbed to the poison. A second control programme was initiated in 1965 when 403 931 zinc phosphide baits (approximately 10 per acre) and 900 traps were used. The idea was to reduce the population of mongooses to 1-2 per square kilometre (i.e. to about 665 on the entire island, against the then estimate of about 82 per square kilometre or a total of 28 373). By the end of a year an estimated 52 000 mongooses had been killed including 9458 trapped. The original population had thus been vastly underestimated. Trapping results indicated that there had been a 55 per cent decrease in the mongoose population in non-forest areas, but a 21 per cent increase in the mountain forests. Repopulation

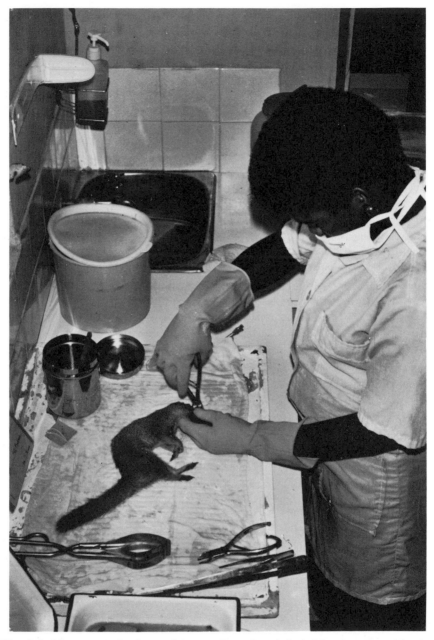

Fig. 6.1. Mongooses in Grenada are collected and their blood analysed in the Medical Research Council laboratory for the presence of rabies serum neutralizing antibodies. This study shows the fruits of a close link between ecological and epizootiological work. (Photograph courtesy of C. R. O. Everard.)

in some areas occurred a few weeks after trapping and poisoning ceased (Everard *et al.* 1974).

During the ten years, 1968–77, mongooses were usually trapped for 5 days a week, 45 weeks a year, and examined for rabies by the fluorescent antibody technique. Since 1973 there has been a decline in the prevalence of trapped-mongoose rabies, with an average incidence of 0.4 per cent in the first 5-year period. This may partly be the result of a mongoose control scheme in 1973, but Everard, James, and Dalres (1979) suspect that it is also because of a natural increase in the number of mongooses with rabies SNA in their blood providing protection from the disease. Everard *et al.* (personal communication) examined 4754 mongooses on Grenada over 4 years (1971–4) and found that 100 (2.1 per cent) were rabid while 498 of 1675 (30 per cent) carried rabies SNA. This proportion increased from 20.8 per cent with rabies SNA in 1971 (when 3.5 per cent of trapped mongooses were rabid) to 43.2 per cent in 1974 (when 0.6 per cent were rabid). This naturally acquired immunity was monitored in 20 mongooses for up to 35 months, after which rabies SNA was still present in all but two of them. In one locality nearly 55 per cent (30 out of 55) of the mongooses had rabies SNA (see Fig. 6.2). There was a significant correlation between a high proportion of mongooses with antibody and a low incidence of rabies and vice versa. This led to the interesting statement by Everard, Race, Price, and Baer (1976): 'Wildlife reduction programs may, therefore, have an adverse effect when neutralizing antibody protected animals are killed indiscriminately, especially if these constitute a high proportion of the population.'

Killing is not only ineffective, but expensive: it costs £80,000 per annum to control 120 km² of Denmark, and Pimental (1955) reported that to trap mongooses cost $364 per square mile, while to poison them sufficiently to achieve a 90 per cent population reduction cost $108 per square mile. Even this high cost is still less than the $208 per fox killed during a post-epizootic control scheme in Tennessee (Lewis 1975). Lewis noted that 'following emergency control programs it has been difficult to determine whether a particular epizootic died down because of population reduction due to control measures, or due to deaths from rabies'. In Eastern Europe and the USSR Adamovich (1978) has also concluded that traditional killing schemes are inadequate. In an area where several vector species are involved and where rabies foci are apparently associated with habitat features rather than vector density *per se* (although it remains uncertain how the two factors reflect each other) Adamovich concludes: 'To control rabies of wild animals one must rely not on extermination of individual animal species in a large territory, but on identification of the elementary foci and changing in

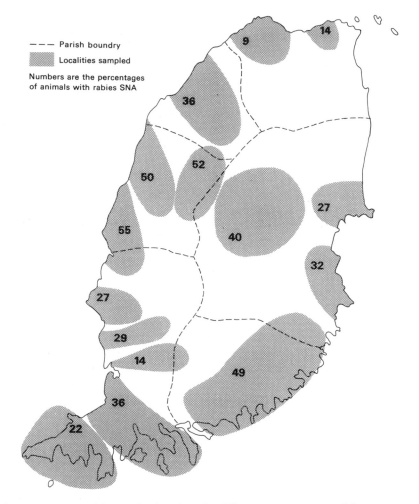

Fig. 6.2. A map of Grenada showing the different percentages of the mongooses in various localities with rabies-serum neutralizing antibodies. The entire population of West Indian mongooses derives from four females and five males introduced to Jamaica in 1872 in an attempt to control rodent pests of sugar cane. Everard (personal communication) suspects that an artificial mongoose-vaccination scheme might boost the population's already high immunity sufficiently to eradicate, or greatly suppress, the disease. (Figure courtesy of C. R. O. Everard.)

them the ecological conditions.' Only two outbreaks in Europe can claim to have been completely eradicated by fox control, one in Dijon in 1923 (where cheese impregnated with strychnine was used as bait) and the other in Corsica in 1943.

Another species which seems to maintain self-contained epizootics is the racoon, *Procyon lotor*. McLean (1975) has described a primary focus of racoon rabies in the south-east United States. Ninety per cent of rabid racoons are reported in Florida and Georgia, where 39 cases a year occur in each state (i.e. more than 60 per cent of all wildlife rabies cases). Racoon rabies is particularly interesting, for it is partly a suburban problem. The issue of urban foxes will be discussed in Chapter 7. The epizootiology of racoon rabies is as imperfectly understood as that of other species: McLean has pointed out the strange fact that in spite of abundant racoons, it was not until 1970 that the disease spread along the gulf coast of Florida from its primary focus. There may be a link between racoons and bat rabies: Constantine (1967) isolated rabies virus from a racoon captured near a Texas bat cave, and the virus resembled that isolated from the Mexican free-tailed bat (*Tadarida brasiliensis*) (see below). Aerosol and oral routes of rabies infection have already been demonstrated, so frequenting bat caves may put racoons and other scavenging predators at risk (Bell and Moore 1971).

As with the mongooses of Grenada, McLean's racoons may have some natural immunity from rabies. He found rabies SNA in 7.2 per cent of racoons in enzootic areas, and between 17 and 22 per cent in epizootic areas. Where the disease occurred only sporadically the frequency of rabies SNA was 2.6 per cent. Of six racoons with antibodies which were captured and kept in a laboratory, 3 still carried them after 2 years, while 3 lost their antibodies after 21 months. McLean hypothesizes that rabies in racoons may involve latent infections, reactivated by stress. He notes ten factors shared by all the racoon rabies epizootics he has studied. They were associated with: (1) dense racoon populations; (2) human habitation; (3) garbage-can feeding; (4) refuse dumps; (5) disturbance and habitat destruction; and (6) coastal habitat. In addition, (7) there was a seasonal peak during winter and early spring; (8) there were high levels of antibody during and after the epizootic; (9) a greater proportion of adult females had detectable rabies SNA; and (10) the epizootics were short-lived.

Of course, many of these factors are likely to be linked, but they led McLean (1975) to suggest that overcrowding in response to rich feeding-sites might create stress through increased contact and competition. He cited the case of an island, Long Boat Key, where, in 1969, an outbreak followed a population build-up of racoons round a feeding site provisioned by a restaurateur. Many mammals can adapt their social systems to highly clumped food supplies (for example, jackals; see Macdonald 1979a) and there is no immediate reason to associate this with undue 'stress'. It would certainly be most interesting to know more about racoon social behaviour, and the limits to its flexibility.

The settlers of early American history were familiar with another carnivore involved in rabies epizooties — the skunk or phobey-cat as it was called. Indeed, settlers carried 'madstones' to ward off skunk-borne rabies. Madstones were hairballs from the stomachs of deer, or gallstones from cattle. The most important source of skunk rabies is the striped skunk, *Mephitis mephitis*; the spotted skunk, *Spilogale spilogale*, accounts for fewer cases. Parker (1975) has reviewed the incidence of skunk rabies. In 1972 skunks accounted for 60 per cent of all wildlife rabies in the USA (2095 skunks and 645 foxes). Although frequently reported rabid, skunks account for rather few human exposures (e.g. 2 per cent in Illinois, Martin *et al.* 1969). Parker associates an increase in skunk rabies with a decline in the fur trade: the skunk pelt harvest of 1950 was 10 per cent of its level in 1940, but in 1948-60 the reports of skunk rabies had increased more than tenfold. Indeed, the incidence of skunk rabies may be greater than is suggested by the figures, since Verts and Storm (1966) note that out of 329 skunks they examined between 1958 and 1964, 30 (9.1 per cent) were rabid, but during those years only two rabid skunks were reported through conventional channels. Verts (1967) has suggested that communal denning may lead to rapid spread of the disease. Infected skunks have high titres of virus in their saliva and a long incubation period (105–177 days) which could, for instance, span the winter. Parker and Wilsnack (1966) showed that skunks may secrete virus for 18 days before death and for up to 8 days prior to the onset of clinical signs of rabies. As mentioned earlier, Johnston and Beauregard (1969) suggest that were it not for a reservoir of skunk rabies, it would be possible to eliminate the disease from the Ontario fox population. In Eastern Europe the polecat and racoon dog may act as reservoirs of rabies and the Siberian polecat, at least, has been found with rabies SNA (Adamovich, 1978).

Another reservoir for rabies in the New World (but not, apparently, in Europe) is bat rabies. This falls into two broad categories: rabies in haematophagous bats of the family Desmodontidae and that in insectivorous and frugivorous bats. Baer (1975) has reviewed the situation for non-haematophagus bats and shows that rabies has been confirmed from a vast array of different species, e.g. more than 30 species in Mexico (where there are over 2000 species of bat in total).

Constantine has worked extensively on bat rabies, especially in the Mexican free-tailed bat. He has described how they live at phenomenal densities with up to 300 per square foot in roosts. Rabies can probably be transmitted between them by aerosol infection, and via maternal milk (Constantine 1967). Adams and Baer (1966) have shown that baby bats frequently cling to each other with their teeth and this may afford an opportunity for rabies transmission; Simms, Allen, and Sulkin (1963)

Fig. 6.3. In parts of North America the distributions of coyotes and of foxes overlap, and both species may be involved in rabies outbreaks. One study in North Dakota is investigating the relationship between the two species, whose ranges seem mutually exclusive. Animals are spotted from the air and driven into dens from which they are dug and equipped with radios. The inset shows biologist Steve Allen marking coyote cubs whose den was located from the air. (Photographs courtesy of S. Allen).

have demonstrated infection of foetuses by transplacental transmission of virus; and Constantine, Solomon, and Woodall (1968) show transplacental transfer of immunity. In 1962 Constantine and his colleagues demonstrated the presence of virus in the olfactory mucosa of a bat and hence demonstrated the possible entry point of an aerosol-communicated infection. Among these bats individuals may recover from rabies. One suggestion is that virus may be stored, between outbreaks, in brown fat and is then released under times of stress or hardship. However, only one case has been found where virus was present in the fat and not elsewhere. The mechanism of periodic outbreak thus needs further research. In contrast to the mild symptoms of rabies in these colonial bats, the disease takes a violent form in some more solitary species (e.g. *Myotis* spp), where its effects on the victim are more like those of rabies in a dog.

In a review of bat rabies, Constantine (1971) considers the possibility of a reservoir of non-virulent rabies amongst carnivores of the sort that he believes to operate among bats. In conclusion he suggests this is entirely credible, with ample opportunity for aerosol transmission during, for instance, aggressive 'spitting' and hissing between mustellid species.

The second category of bats involved in the spread of rabies are the vampires. Vampire bats feed on blood, principally from cattle. Acha (1967) has reviewed the incidence of both bat and bovine rabies and quotes the economic losses involved at over $250 million annually. He also points out that vampire bats transmit equine trypanosomiases. Linhart (1975) has reviewed methods used to reduce these losses, which include attacks on bat colonies with weapons ranging from flame-throwers through dynamite to various fumigants. In Colombia bats were deliberately infected with Newcastle disease, which completely annihilated 5000 in 6 days, but seems a most dangerous enterprise. Linhart describes how bat-bite wounds on cattle were treated with strychnine syrup to poison bats returning for a second meal: 661 bats were killed after painting 4288 cows in this way. Mist netting of bats can reduce their numbers locally by 70–80 per cent. Two ideas have been tested recently to reduce vampire-bat numbers more effectively. Linhart, Flores Crespo, and Mitchell (1972) painted a slow-acting poison (chlorophacinone) in petroleum jelly on to the backs of mist-netted vampires. The anointed bats were released and returned to their roosts where their companions groomed them clean and were thus poisoned. Each treated bat resulted in the death of 34 others and one such trial resulted in a 95–98 per cent reduction in the incidence of bat bites on cows. Another trial resulted in a reduction in bat bites of over 80 per cent, which lasted for at least 27 months. Linhart *et al.* (1972) stress the specificity of this technique which involves no risk to non-target species of bats.

Thompson, Mitchell, and Burns (1972) have developed a different, but also specific, approach. They capitalize on the differential sensitivity of vampires and cattle to an anticoagulant called diphenadione. This drug is injected into a cow, which can readily tolerate a dose of 5.0 mg/kg. A bat is susceptible to only 1.0 mg/kg and so succumbs on attacking the cow. On a sample of 207 cows the incidence of bites fell from 1.1 bites per cow to 0.07 bites per cow after two weeks of this treatment (a 93 per cent improvement).

Both these methods involve slaughtering large numbers of bats, which is regrettable, but they have the merit of specificity and they appear to be effective. In these respects they differ from most attempts to control carnivore rabies in both North America and Europe. The presence of many vectors, of which some acquire natural immunity, clearly complicate the epidemiology of the disease.

In Britain red deer in Richmond Park were the only wild species involved in an outbreak in 1918. That outbreak resulted from a breach of the quarantine regulations. A pet dog was smuggled into the country and the consequences took three years to remedy: there were 319 animal cases in 17 counties of England and Wales and 144 people who were bitten were given Pasteur treatment. Although the dog was smuggled into Plymouth in mid-May, the disease was not suspected until late August. By that time some 20 dogs, having turned mysteriously savage, had been destroyed already and rabid dogs were found wandering 30–40 miles from home. Hole (1969) uses this as a forceful argument in favour of UK quarantine regulations (pointing out incidentally, that 7 of 35 cases of rabies diagnosed in quarantine between 1918 and 1969 developed symptoms after the fourth month of detention; the dog that caused the Camberley outbreak in 1969 had actually served six months' quarantine). Just as Hole has reported the real consequences of un-detected dog rabies, so P. Bacon (1980) has considered the possible consequences of undetected fox rabies. Using European data that suggest that only a tiny proportion of rabid foxes are reported, he has shown that if, for example, only 5 per cent of rabid foxes are spotted, then the number of foxes infected and the spread of the disease before it is recognized can be calculated for a given level of certainty that a rabid fox will be found. In this case, 45 foxes might have been infected and the disease spread radially 9–32 km during 3–4 months before it could be certain of detection at a probability of 90 per cent. If reporting was even worse, say 2 per cent as estimated by Braunschweig (1980), and if 99 per cent certainty of detection was demanded, then 228 foxes might have been infected during the 7 months before detection in which the epizooty would have spread up to 56 km radially. Bacon uses these calculations to emphasize the importance of enforcing quarantine regulations.

7 Alternative methods

In earlier chapters I have described some of the models underlying current rabies-control schemes. In 1975 William Winkler and his colleagues wrote of these, 'For many years attempts to control sylvatic rabies in wild carnivore populations were based on lowering population densities to remove infected animals and to reduce intraspecies transmission. This approach has not proven adequate' (Winkler, McLean, and Cowart 1975). This statement is clearly supported by much of the evidence presented earlier, but what other possibilities exist? One is to immunize wild foxes in the field, perhaps building up a cordon of rabies-resistant foxes round infected areas. Discounting the practical difficulties, this seems a very attractive idea since it might not only subtly exploit the foxes' behaviour (for example, by letting territorial behaviour limit fox movements) but also seems to reduce human meddling in the ecosystem. On the last point it is necessary to remember that rabies is a natural controlling factor for many fox populations. If it is in our interest to remove this factor from fox population dynamics, for our safety, should we regard this as anticonservationist? This type of question leads to the complex issue of the ethics of wildlife management, touched on by Macdonald and Boitani (1979). In any event, the weight of evidence suggests that fox populations would rapidly be limited by food if a vaccination scheme did eliminate rabies. But, is vaccination a realistic proposition? Before discussing this I shall briefly digress to describe the types of vaccine which are already available.

Louis Pasteur was the first man to treat successfully a person bitten by a rabid animal. He had worked previously with anthrax and had discovered that by culturing the disease organism artificially in a meat broth it lost its virulence after several generations. When this non-virulent strain of anthrax was injected into animals they did not develop the disease, but they did develop a protection against later infection by the virulent bacterium. Live viruses made into vaccines in this way are known as 'attentuated' or 'fixed' and it was such a virus that Pasteur used to innoculate a nine-year-old boy from Alsace called Joseph Meister in 1885. The boy had been bitten by a rabid dog and Pasteur injected him with a vaccine made from the infected spinal cord of a rabbit and dried over caustic potash for two weeks. Pasteur's treatment was successful and the boy survived; the virus Pasteur used had been passaged through the brains of ninety rabbits. The resulting 'fixed' virus was injected into a rabbit and when it died a segment of its spinal cord was dried for ten days. Similar sections of cord were dried for progressively shorter times, producing successively less attentuated viruses. The first dose injected during post-exposure treatment was the most attentuated virus, and on subsequent days more potent batches were used. The patient's body responds by developing antibodies to combat the virus. By 1886 Pasteur could report 349 successes out of 350 cases treated. Nowadays about one-and-a-half million people are vaccinated annually and, as Turner (1977) has pointed out, for most of them the treatment is little different from that prepared originally by Pasteur. In fact in 1898 the Pasteur Institute showed 96 deaths amongst 20 166 people treated. This 0.46 per cent failure rate compares with 0.5 per cent failure of treatment in India today (see Steele 1975).

Recent advances in vaccine preparation have been reviewed by Crick and Brown (1976). In 1911 Semple, working in India, produced a vaccine from nervous tissue in which the virus had been killed by incubating it with carbolic acid; nowadays inactivated or dead virus preparations form a second major category of vaccines. Inactivated viruses cultured in nervous tissue, such as the brain, are injected into the patient in quantities that are miniscule in comparison with the amount of brain tissue injected. In fact, during 14 to 21 days of post-exposure treatment a patient receives an estimated 2.5 g of brain. It is this that accounts for the well-known risk attendant on post-exposure treatment, since the patient's body reacts against this enormous injection of foreign protein (1 in 11 000 people die from vaccine reactions). The most dangerous protein is myelin (which acts as an insulating material round nerves in a way similar to the rubber coating on electrical wiring). Myelin has not formed round the nerves of new-born mammals and it was this fact that gave rise to the preparation of 'suckling mouse' vaccine in the 1950s (by Fuenzalida). The risk attached to using suckling mouse or rat vaccine is only a fraction of that attached to using adult brain. Nevertheless, Semple had a failure rate of only 0.19 per cent out of 2009 cases of Europeans treated in India.

Most people vaccinated against rabies in the United Kingdom since 1957 will have received an inactivated vaccine developed by Powell and Culbertson from viruses grown in duck embryos (duck-embryo vaccine, DEV). DEV is almost free from neurological side-effects although patients allergic to egg protein can suffer severe reactions. It is used both for immunizing people likely to contact rabies and for post-exposure treatment.

Other vaccines are prepared in laboratory tissue cultures, rather than in live hosts (first done in 1936 by Webster and Clow). Fenje produced one of these (ERA, after Evelyn, Rotitnicki, and Abelseth) in 1960 using virus from a rabid dog. This may be cultured in hamster or pig kidney cells. Another live virus vaccine is the Flury strain (named after the girl from whom it was isolated in 1948). Two varieties of Flury vaccine are made, distinguished by the number of passages through chick embryos. LEP (low egg passage, 50 chicks) is used effectively to immunize dogs while HEP (high egg passage, nearly 200 chicks) is used for cats and puppies.

Most recently attention has been directed towards the so-called human diploid-cell vaccine (HDCV) which is prepared from vaccines cultured in human cells (see Aoki, Tyrell and Hill 1974). HDCV may replace all its predecessors. In the UK it is now the recommended pre-exposure vaccine and is used together with anti-rabies serum in the treatment of post-exposure cases. HDCV is expensive to produce and will probably be a luxury of the developed countries for the foreseeable future.

In summary, the patient, human or otherwise, may be immunized after being bitten and before developing symptoms. This is possible because of the long delay between infection and incubation of the disease, which may be due to proliferation of virus at the site of the bite (Murphy and Bauer 1974). The delay allows time for immunity, stimulated by the vaccine, to build up before the symptoms of the disease develop. Post-exposure treatment always involves inoculation with anti-rabies serum (containing antibodies from the blood of other animals) together with vaccine during the first 24 hours of infection. Turner (1977) points to the value of using serum in conjunction with vaccine, and quotes an example where a rabid wolf in Iran bit 29 people. Of these victims a proportion had severe head wounds; half these patients were treated with vaccine alone while the other half were treated with vaccine and anti-rabies serum. Seventy-five per cent of those receiving only vaccine died compared with 14 per cent of those receiving both.

Returning now to the possibilities of immunizing wild foxes against rabies, it is clearly only pre-exposure vaccination which is relevant. The reason for exploring this idea and expressing dissatisfaction with present schemes is because mass-killing has generally not worked, and *not* because 'We live in a faint-hearted world over-saturated with the idea of conservation' (Henderson and White 1978).

Nevertheless, J. Berger (personal communication) speculates that in West Germany there may be an association between areas of rabies resurgence and conservationists' activities, such that where fox numbers are encouraged to increase the disease reappears.

First, it is necessary to persuade the foxes to vaccinate themselves. The idea of an oral vaccine for use on foxes against rabies was first given serious consideration by Baer, Linhart, and Dean in 1963 and pursued further by Baer, Abelseth and Debbie in 1970. The initial results were not clear-cut. Some foxes were given vaccine via gastric tubes (both the

CVS (challenge virus standard) strain of fixed virus and the LEP vaccine); others were given subcutaneous inoculation (with Semple vaccine). On challenge with rabies virus all the foxes fed LEP vaccine, and 4 of 5 treated with CVS virus, died of rabies. Two of the 5 inoculated with Semple vaccine also died. However, 1 fox fed CVS virus and 3 in-oculated with Semple vaccine developed antibodies and all of these immunized 40 out of 53 foxes with ERA while Mayr, Kraft, Jaeger, and Haacke (1972) were unsuccessful with attentuated virus in drinking water. Thereafter, George Baer and his colleagues at the Centre for Disease Control of the Public Health Service in Georgia have continued to explore the idea. In 1975 Baer, Broderson, and Yeger conducted a series of experiments to confirm that foxes had been immunized by the strict oral route. In their experiments foxes were fistulated so that vaccine was introduced directly into the stomach. Another group of foxes was then treated by dropping 1 ml of liquid vaccine on to the tongue and buccal mucosa (the membranes lining the mouth). Serum was later collected from the foxes and tested for rabies-neutralizing antibodies which indicated that the vaccination had been successful (the vaccine was the ERA strain BHK 21). After 13 weeks the surviving foxes were killed and the brains of all the experimental foxes were examined by the fluorescent antibody test for signs of rabies viruses.

These experiments indicated that vaccination could not be effected through the stomach but it could be by the virus being absorbed into tissues of the mouth. Thus to vaccinate foxes orally in the field they had to be given the vaccine in a bait in such a way that guaranteed that it would be spread round the mouth rather than being swallowed whole. Winkler *et al.* (1975) found that 15 of 36 foxes fed on baits impregnated with modified live virus (ERA BHK 21) developed serum rabies-neutralizing antibody. The vaccine was fed to captive foxes on dog biscuits in wax mixed with beef tallow and sardine oil (to make them both tasty and waterproof). These authors concluded that the application of this technique to wild animals was promising.

Baer and his colleagues unearthed two further problems concerning the possibility of vaccination. The vaccine used was unstable: at temperatures greater than about 4 °C it deteriorates in a matter of hours; unless it can be stabilized, the foxes would be required to eat the bait with improbable rapidity. Perhaps the biggest problem, however, was that there were indications that a vaccine which effectively immunized the foxes against disease might actually produce at least a mild form of the disease, if eaten by other species such as cotton rats. This represented the most serious hurdle to the possibility of actually using this technique in practice, since the risk of infection of non-target species was unacceptable. For example, while safety testing an oral vaccine Winkler *et al.*

(1975) had found that one of ten cotton rats fed a massive dose of liquid vaccine had died of rabies. Admittedly other cotton rats, opossums, foxes, and hamsters had all survived huge doses of intramuscularly injected vaccine, but the risk of vaccine-induced rabies could not be dismissed. In 1976 Winkler reported that when MLU vaccine was fed to foxes it successfully immunized them, but when fed to rodents it could infect up to half of them with the disease, although only 17 per cent eventually died. When fatal infection occurred virus was found in the victim's salivary glands and hence the possibility of passing on infection existed. Wachendörfer and Förster (1976) have studied whether the pathogenicity of vaccine to non-target species could be reduced if the virus were more highly modified. They passaged virus 80 times in canine kidney cells and still found residual parthogenicity after oral application for 6 out of 11 species. It remains unknown whether vaccine-induced rabies could maintain a chain of infection in the wild, during which its initially low virulence might be increased. We have to remember that foxes can not only be immunized orally but they can also be infected by the same route by eating rabid prey (Kovalev, Sedov, and Shashenko 1971; Bell and Moore 1971) — although this seems more likely to affect young foxes (Ramsden and Johnston 1975).

Work continued on the possibility of oral vaccination at the Centre for Disease Control, and in 1976 Winkler and Baer reported the results of a successful attempt to immunize red foxes against rabies using a sausage bait which had been 'cored' to permit the insertion of a plastic tube 11 cm long and 0.5 cm in diameter containing 2 ml of vaccine. Foxes were fed these sausages containing two different vaccines whose efficiency was being compared and then, after 21 or 31 weeks these foxes, and others which had not been fed the sausage baits, were challenged with virus from the salivary glands of a rabid wild fox. After 60 days the surviving foxes were killed and their brains and salivary gland tissue tested for infectious rabies virus. The results were encouraging: all the control animals which had not had the opportunity of being immunized through eating sausage bait died of rabies, but those animals fed on one of the two vaccines survived. (Again, the most effective vaccine was ERA virus grown on BHK-21 cells.) They also tested the stability of the vaccine and found that it was still potent after 30 days at -20 to $+4\,°C$. But at more than $+25\,°C$ it lost potency in 5–10 days. This could be improved by adding a 'stabilizing' chemical. The sausage bait worked, but the mechanism of getting vaccine on to the buccal and pharyngeal mucosa remained cumbersome. During the trials drips of vaccine were seen to be lost as the foxes chewed. The tubes were therefore filled with surplus vaccine so that there was a better chance of some coming into contact with the mucosal membranes. Debbie, Baer, Andralouis,

Shaddock, and Moore (1979) have since reported on a vaccine which immunizes by the enteric route, that is it can be absorbed through the intestine; furthermore, it seems that this vaccine is safe in terms of not infecting other species. The way is now open for its use in the field where the temperature is low enough to prevent the vaccine from deteriorating. Debbie's experiments were carried out with a strain of modified live rabies virus called Street Alabama Dufferin (SAD). The vaccine is sprayed on to sugar granules (2 mm in diameter) and is then coated with methylcellulose to prevent premature digestion in the stomach. There are considerable technical problems in preparing this enteric vaccine, but so far it has been fed, in meat baits, to foxes, skunks, racoons, dogs, and mongooses and has immunized at least one of each species. Practical problems remain in perfecting this technique, but these should be soluble.

Many problems are common to both oropharyngeal and intestinal vaccination. The liquid or powder (lyophilized) vaccine must be produced cheaply, presented to foxes in some small, inconspicuous form in acceptable bait and it must be safe for non-target species. It must also be stable out of doors under all weather conditions. Foxes are adept at picking 'foreign' lumps out of bait and so the vaccine capsule must not be readily detectable. At the same time, for the oral route, the vaccine must be released into direct contact with the mucosal tissue of the mouth and pharynx.

Many of the problems encountered in attempting to vaccinate wild foxes orally are similar to those that have already been studied with the aim of poisoning foxes. Trials to find the most suitable baits and the optimum baiting strategem for a poisoning campaign should be easily modified for an oral vaccination campaign. Field trials employing marked bait have enabled estimates to be made of how many foxes might be vaccinated (or poisoned) using given baiting regimes. The principle is to mark the bait with a chemical which can later be detected in the animal which has eaten it (a so-called biomarker). One good example is the antibiotic tetracycline, which is deposited eventually in calciferous tissue such as teeth (Linhart and Kennelly 1967; Ellenton and Johnston 1975). Using this technique Ministry of Agriculture biologists in Wales have carried out baiting trials in a 20-km^2 area in spring. They prebaited with one marker for 10 days and then used marked bait for two days. They then killed 65 foxes within the study area (i.e. 3 foxes/km^2) and found that 55 per cent had eaten marked food during the prebait period and 412 during the two-day mock-poisoning period. During a second trial they obtained a similar success rate (Lloyd, personal communication). In the course of these trials they discovered some practical difficulties. Using rabbit and fish baits in Pembrokeshire they found that acceptance of bait was significantly worse during June, July and early August (the period when Wachendörfer had most success in Germany with baited chickens' heads). They also found that baits were more readily taken on headlands rather than from fields. From experience of watching foxes I should certainly expect baits to be more readily discovered along hedgerows or traditional fox paths than if they were laid out on a regular grid. Trials along railways have been very successful, with almost 100 per cent acceptance of bait. The general finding of studies on baiting, as summarized by the World Health Organization, is that uptake varies from 5–75 per cent during 4–14 days after baiting. In West Germany Manz (1975) reported bait acceptance of 60–70 per cent, independent of fox density. One problem with baiting relates to the details of fox behaviour: in common with many other predators that face the problems of day-to-day fluctuations in the availability of prey, foxes are inclined to store any surplus food they can get for times of food shortage. They do this by caching surplus food in holes dug in the ground. The prey may be stored there for several days before the fox returns to eat it (Macdonald 1976). Indeed, the choice of bait in which to present vaccine is complicated in itself, since foxes behave differently towards different prey species. They are more likely to cache surplus food if it is a preferred item in the diet, and are thereafter more likely to return to caches which contain preferred food (Macdonald 1977*b*).

David Johnston has carried out extensive trials in Canada, with a view to using oral vaccination to stop the epizootic described in Chapter 4 (Johnston and Beauregard 1969). His plan is to use modified live virus in baits distributed over 30 000 square miles. He estimated originally that a bait density of 150/square mile might be necessary. Recent successes suggest, however, that 60–90 baits/linear mile of aircraft baiting could vaccinate 74 per cent of foxes. The main problem is to vaccinate skunks as well as foxes, for there are indications that skunks are the reservoir for the disease. MacInnes and Johnston (1975) have described preliminary results of this study. They overcame the problem of storing freeze-dried vaccine in the field by hanging it from trees in beef-scented hermetically sealed plastic bags which the fox then pulls open. The dried vaccine is sticky and hence cannot be gulped down before coming in contact with the mouth or pharynx. Foxes are more likely to take heavy food items than featherlight ones, and so Johnston found that adding a sterilized stone to the bait bag increased his success rate from 3 per cent to 80 per cent.

Johnston and Voigt (unpublished data) have recently explored the practicability of distributing bait on a large scale. They have air-dropped thousands of baits over a large area in order to discover what proportion of the fox population would take them and hence what probability there was of attaining an adequate level of immunity in the population as a whole. Each bait was treated with a biomarker drug, which when eaten left a trace in the fox's teeth indicating the day on which it ate the bait. By liaison with hunters Johnston was able to recover the teeth of dead foxes killed within his study area and thereafter to test for the presence of his marker drug and hence calculate the proportion of foxes which had taken the bait. Not only were the results sufficiently encouraging to suggest that mass vaccination of the entire population was feasible, but the estimated cost (at 1976 prices) of getting each fox to eat a bait was in the order of 6 cents — a figure which compares more than favourably with the current cost of killing foxes.

Voigt (personal communication) reports that all ages and sexes of foxes are marked equally effectively by the biomarker baits, and hence would be as effectively reached by the vaccine. He notes one example where a fox was shot after eating a marked bait for the third successive year. So, had the baits contained vaccine, that fox could have been successfully vaccinated each year. The current cost of rabies to Ontario is probably in excess of $4.6 million per annum, and the initial costs of oral vaccination could be just as much. However, the ecological advantages and long-term rewards of vaccination could sway this balance. In fact, fox-fur trapping is of major economic importance to the state and would benefit from any increase in fox numbers if rabies were drastically reduced.

The baiting strategy and the success rate of 74 per cent (only about 40 per cent of skunks) which Johnston achieved is, of course, appropriate only to the Canadian habitat and fox population structure (approximately 1 fox per 2.6 sq km), but the results of ground baiting trials in the UK and Germany are all favourable. Figure 7.1 presents a summary of the success with which Johnston's team have achieved bait acceptance averaged for several trials in three study areas for four species. They found that, at least for juvenile foxes, maximum bait uptake had been achieved by just over two weeks from the time of first bait placement. In summary, advances in both immunology and baiting techniques make field vaccination campaigns feasible for the near future. Unfortunately, oral or enteric vaccination has been successful only with attenuated live-virus preparations, and the World Health Organization has expressed fears about the pathogenicity of live-virus vaccine in non-target species. Effective screening is certainly crucial to ensure that such risks are obviated. Thus, ironically, Johnston and his coworkers have devised a highly effective delivery system with nothing as yet to deliver. It nevertheless seems likely that an appropriate enterically coated vaccine will be developed soon. One problem is making a coating for the

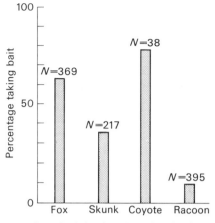

Fig. 7.1. Preliminary results of trials aimed at developing maximal bait acceptance by rabies vectors in Ontario, Canada. (Data from D. H. Johnston.) Now sausage baits are dropped in plastic bags which attract foxes, act as a chamber to generate odour, and yield diagnostic tooth marks of the species which ate the bait.

vaccine which will pass through the stomach before it dissolves to liberate the vaccine which can then be absorbed in the intestine. Design of suitable coating thus requires knowing about pH changes down the alimentary canal. With this knowledge the vaccine coating could be designed to dissolve at the appropriate pH. This type of information can probably be fairly readily obtained using a radio-pill swallowed by the fox and whose signal varied according to the surrounding pH. In Britain, which is free of rabies, live vaccines are judged unacceptable for animal use. (See the Waterhouse Report (1971), which is also an excellent source of other information on rabies.)

If oral vaccination is technically feasible, what practical effects could it have? In practice, Johnston and Voigt would answer this by continued biomarker studies during vaccination. In theory Berger (1976) has tried to answer the question with a simulation model. His principal question was what proportion of a fox population must be vaccinated to stop the epizootic, and is this proportion practically attainable? He constructed a model based on 6 × 15 grid squares (1 km² each), set the density of foxes in each at between 0 and 5 and scattered 180 'foxes' randomly on the grids to give a mean density of 3 foxes/km². Berger used frequency distribution of latent periods and infectious periods with means of 29.9 days and 7.9 days respectively and calculated a susceptibility factor for each fox. He also assigned various probabilities for foxes to move in various directions across the grid. Berger found that by 'allowing' each infectious fox one contact per day he simulated an

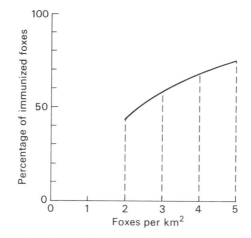

Fig. 7.2. The immunization schedule required to prevent a rabies epidemic in relation to fox population density according to the model derived by Berger. (After Berger 1976.)

epizootic which spread (across his very small grid) at a speed close to reality and so he selected this otherwise arbitrary contact rate. Using all these variables he simulated the weekly incidence of disease on populations of different densities and with different proportions immunized. Figure 7.2 presents his results. At high fox densities Berger found that almost 80 per cent of the population had to be immunized to stop the epizootic, but 70 per cent immunity slowed its spread. For this reason he recommended that vaccination alone would be inadequate at high fox densities, and so should be used in conjunction with hunting under these circumstances.

Mollison (personal communication) criticizes this type of model on the grounds that it employs more subtle variables than necessary to achieve the same result and that it is impossible to resolve which of these variables is exerting important influences. He uses Berger's figures to show that the proportion of animals infected can be predicted solely from the reproduction rate of the disease (see p. 80), and claims that when the reproduction rate falls below about 1.5 the epizootic must be curtailed. The reproduction rate is the number of animals a rabid animal infects before he dies. To keep the epizootic going it has to be greater than unity, since some of the animals the rabid animal infects will already be rabid. The reproduction rate R is calculated by multiplying the number of susceptible animals N by the infection rate β and dividing by the duration of the infectious period γ: i.e. $R = N\beta/\gamma$ (Bailey 1975). If vaccination or any other process removes enough susceptible animals from the population so that, with a short infectious period, each rabid fox does not have time before it dies to infect another, then R will fall below unity and the epizootic will die out. Mollison argues that the inclusion of variables other than N, β, and γ does not affect the final conclusion.

If the authorities judge live-virus vaccines to be unsafe for use on stock in the UK and even less safe for use in vaccinating foxes in the field, and if killing seems generally unsatisfactory on the Continent, then what options exist if rabies reaches British shores?

First, it is imperative to realize that the British situation is quite different to that in continental Europe: the problem in Britain would be to prevent the proliferation of a new outbreak, rather than to combat an already endemic disease. There would be more immediate hope of success in this aim than one might expect in tackling endemic rabies. It is for this reason that Ministry of Agriculture biologists in Britain argue that very extreme action could be justified if rabies did reach our shores; the cost of failure could be enormous. Lloyd (1977) has very fully explained the factors leading to the Ministry's current contingency plans. Before going into these, it is worth mentioning that the risk of the problem arising may be very slight: certainly selfish people will continue to smuggle pets into the country, but for rabies to reach British wildlife several improbable conditions would have to be satisfied: a smuggled dog must develop rabies; it, or one of its victims, must make contact with a fox, which it must then catch and bite; the fox must then develop the disease. Foxes normally avoid dogs at all costs (although one hears of very rare friendly liaisons), but cats may be more of a risk. I have frequently watched cats and foxes together in suburban settings, where they have either ignored each other, or the cats have been antagonistic towards the fox. I have never seen a direct fight or attack as foxes have invariably fled at the slightest sign of feline hostility. However, cats do occasionally feature in fox diet (e.g. Barnonvskya and Kolosov 1935), and Harris (personal communication) has found this in London too, although most of the cats there may have been scavanged road casualties. Nevertheless, if British cats were infected with rabies there could be a serious risk of transmission to foxes. There are many feral cats living 'wild' around British towns. One recent survey (P. Rees, personal communication) of 85 colonies found that 68 per cent were in hospital grounds and that 42 per cent of the colonies numbered under ten animals, but 12 per cent numbered over 50. Male cats could pose particular problems, for their ranges may be ten times as large as those of their females, and hence they could spread the disease between neighbouring colonies (Macdonald and Apps 1978). There is also contact between foxes and badgers in and around towns. I recently watched

Fig. 7.3. In spite of fears to the contrary foxes rarely threaten cats around human dwellings; in fact cats frequently chase foxes away. However, the nightly contact between these two species would present a major problem for rabies control in Britain where populations of both are high around towns. (Photograph courtesy of D. W. Macdonald and M. T. Newdick.)

a sow badger furiously chasing a well-grown fox cub around a garden on the outskirts of Oxford and it is not uncommon to see foxes 'pestering' badgers while they forage for earthworms. Thus there is plenty of scope for contact, and potentially for disease transmission, between all these species. So, while the risk of rabies ever reaching British foxes may be very small, it is a real fear and it is vital to have valid contingency plans.

The British government's official policy is summarized in a memorandum published by the Ministry of Agriculture, Fisheries, and Food (MAFF) (1977), which states two aims:

(a) The primary aim: to keep rabies out of Great Britain by means of stringent import controls, compulsory quarantine requirements, severe penalties for offenders and the active awareness support of the public.
(b) The contingency aim: should an outbreak nevertheless occur, to contain it and to stamp it out swiftly and effectively before it takes hold.

To facilitate these aims responsibility for different aspects is allocated to various departments ranging from Customs and Excise to the Department of the Environment which are aided by five legislative facilities: (1) The Rabies Act, 1974: outlines penalties for offences; (2) The Rabies (Importation of Dogs, Cats and Other Mammals) Order 1974: outlines import controls and quarantine restrictions; (3) The Rabies (Control) Order 1974: strategy in the event of an outbreak; (4) The Rabies (Compensation) Order, 1976: compensation for compulsory destruction of livestock; (5) The Rabies (Importation of Dogs, Cats and Other Mammals) (Amendment) Order 1977: increasing the stringency and effectiveness of the 1974 Order.

The enactment of these laws has so far been confined to infringements concerning domestic animals. In 1975 there were 52 prosecutions with an average fine of £175 (up from £50 in 1974). In 1976 there were 125 prosecutions of which 88 offenders were foreign nationals. One hundred and eleven of the cases were either dogs or cats. Five offenders received prison sentences (3–4 months) with fines of up to £400 in magistrates' courts and £1000 in Crown courts, with an overall average of £124.

These figures can be seen in the perspective of the magnitude of international animal traffic. In 1975 3758 dogs and 1215 cats were legally imported into Britain, and 143 dogs and 38 cats were known to be landed illegally. In 1976 the ratio of illegal to legal imports was 118:4258 for dogs and 45:1595 for cats. The recent official stringency in this area seems to be effective. Part of the improvement may also result from the Government's annually escalating rabies-awareness campaigns.

What provisions exist for a rabies outbreak in wildlife? The MAFF memorandum states: 'In the event of a rabies outbreak in wildlife anywhere in Great Britain, control measures would concentrate on the destruction of foxes in the infected area. The methods employed would be those calculated to be most effective to suit local circumstances, while presenting the minimum hazard to other species of wildlife and to farm and domestic animals.'

This statement embraces two critical issues: (1) which 'effective' methods, and (2) how large an 'infected area'?

Lloyd (1977) has listed the criteria that a control method must satisfy to be acceptable. These include producing a significant reduction in the fox population, not involving the use of dogs, being effective at all seasons and applicable to many habitats, requiring little skill, and causing little harassment to the fox population. He concludes that only poisoning satisfies sufficient criteria. It is for this reason that Lloyd and his colleagues have conducted the research on bait acceptance described earlier. They believe that the optimum strategy would be to prebait for a number of days until bait acceptance reached a maximum and then to introduce poison into the baits for two further days.

The area throughout which the bait would be distributed would to some extent be influenced by the time of the year and habitat, but would probably be a circle of radius about 12 miles (19 km) (as schematized by the Office of Health Economics 1976, p. 23). If an outbreak occurred in summer when fox populations contain few itinerant animals, the circle might be as small as 13 km radius. An area of 1230 km² (500 square miles) might be supplied with 10 000 bait stations. The aim of this scheme would be to kill quickly any infected foxes *before* the disease got a foothold. The poison would be aimed at the handful of foxes infected in the first days of an outbreak.

The poison baits would be distributed within a chequerboard pattern of 1-km squares, each baited square receiving at least 30 baits (each in an area of about 40 hectares). On this pattern the furthest distance from an unbaited point to the nearest poison would be about 625 m. Some fox home ranges have a diameter smaller than this distance, although probably not in agricultural habitats. This scheme would require considerable man-power (an estimated 120 people in the field) and take about 1 week to set up and 26–27 days to complete the poisoning exercise. It is hoped that the poison could be biodegradable so that after 4–5 days in the field it would lose its potency; such a poison could be safer and more humane than strychnine. It seems highly likely that 20–30 per cent of foxes would escape poisoning. If some of these were rabid and they spread the disease then further 'fire-brigade' actions would probably be pointless unless the outbreak were in a geographically isolatable region, such as the south-west peninsula.

The chances of killing the right foxes with such a scheme must vary hugely with fox density, for the baited zone might conceivably contain about a hundred or over five thousand fox territories (and more individuals) according to the habitat in question (Macdonald 1977c). Nevertheless, as Lloyd (1977, p. 95) writes 'drastic action . . . would be justified by the penalties of failure'. If rabies reached British wildlife and if the planned drastic action failed to eliminate it within a matter of days, there would seem to be little virtue in pursuing a fox-killing scheme thereafter (see p. 113 on consequences of missing a rabid fox). The evidence from the Continent would suggest that population reduction is so inadequate that we should look immediately for alternatives, and the possibility of oral vaccination of wild foxes seems to be the obvious candidate.

Although little thought has been given to it so far, I believe that an integrated combination of methods could be effective in eliminating endemic rabies. Where foci of an epizootic exist, killing zones could be surrounded by a belt of immunized foxes. Killing and vaccinating schemes could also be integrated seasonally to reduce the possibilities of

Fig. 7.4. A church wall provides a safe vantage point for an urban-dwelling fox in Oxford to watch the passing traffic. (Photograph, using an image intensifier, courtesy of N. G. Hough.)

disease transmission to the optimal minimum. In this context P. Bacon (personal communication) has suggested that a sterilization scheme might also be usefully integrated into a rabies-control programme.

Much discussion of possible problems of rabies control in Great Britain has centred around the behaviour of urban foxes. It is common knowledge that many towns in Britain are populated by foxes. London has a large fox population (Teagle 1967; Harris 1977) and here the foxes seem prone to road accidents, with 32.4 per cent of 256 adult foxes in one sample showing signs of old fractures (Harris 1978*b*). Little is known about the behaviour of foxes in urban habitats, but considering the variation that exists between other habitats it is reasonable to presume that fox behaviour in towns will vary in some respects from that in other environs. Under the auspices of the Nature Conservancy Council, S. Harris, M. Newdick, and I have collaborated on a comparative study of the behaviour of foxes in Oxford and Bristol. This work is still in its infancy, but in view of its relevance here, a few preliminary remarks may be of interest. Figure 7.6 shows the approximate home-ranges of several

Fig. 7.5. A radio-tagged fox, viewed through an image intensifier, in Oxford's city centre. A combination of radio tracking, direct observations, and questionnaire surveys has shown that foxes harmlessly inhabit almost every part of the city (Macdonald and Newdick, unpublished data).

radio-tracked foxes in and around Oxford. Foxes have been seen in almost every urban habitat in Oxford, ranging from terraced houses to the university grounds. One earth has been excavated under the University's Astrophysics department and into the housing of a seismograph (which reported unexpected tremors). Figure 7.7 depicts the habitat of the most urban foxes we have found in Oxford, where one family, in particular one cub, spent much time within a large industrial warehouse. The cub slept inside storage bins, favouring those containing more comfortable items such as carpets, and played with paper balls thrown by men on the night-shift. Our data are too few to comment on the social organization of these urban foxes, other than to note from Fig. 7.6 that some home-ranges overlap almost completely, whereas others are largely exclusive. This may indicate similarities with the strictly territorial family group system pictured in Fig. 4.5 (p. 49) but if so, borders are apparently not so rigorously defined. On

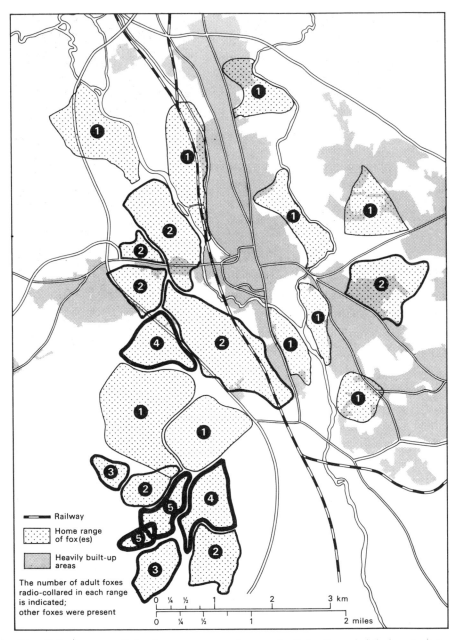

Fig. 7.6. A map of the home-ranges of several of the foxes radio-tracked in Oxford during a study which is still in its infancy. The range sizes are greater than some found on the outskirts of the town (see Fig. 4.5) and provisionally suggest a territorial system. We have found evidence of several adult foxes within certain home-ranges but their social relationships are as yet unknown. Only the approximate borders of the home-ranges are shown so their positions given here should not be taken as an indicator of the social organization of the foxes. (From an as yet uncompleted study by D. W. Macdonald and M. T. Newdick.)

Fig. 7.7. The capture for tagging of a juvenile fox residing in an industrial warehouse. (Photograph courtesy of M. T. Newdick.)

this question of the exclusiveness of fox home-ranges (or territories) it is worth mentioning that in several areas neighbouring ranges overlap appreciably. In some cases the overlap seems to be in habitat which is unimportant from a feeding standpoint. For example, I have followed two neighbouring families who slept in the same wood (but in different earths) but whose nightly foraging never overlapped at all. Similarly, T. von Schantz (personal communication) has told me of a case of overlap where the shared habitat was of worse food quality than the exclusive parts. Much more work should be done on the pattern of availability of fox food in different habitats and on the configuration of home-ranges with respect to this pattern.

Another point to emerge from Fig. 7.6 is that some fox home-ranges span both town and country. This has led us to distinguish between city-dwelling foxes and 'commuters'. Some animals clearly sleep by day in the countryside and move into the town at night. This continuity between town and country is also seen in the behaviour of itinerant foxes. One yearling male fox we radio-collared in Oxford City on 6 April

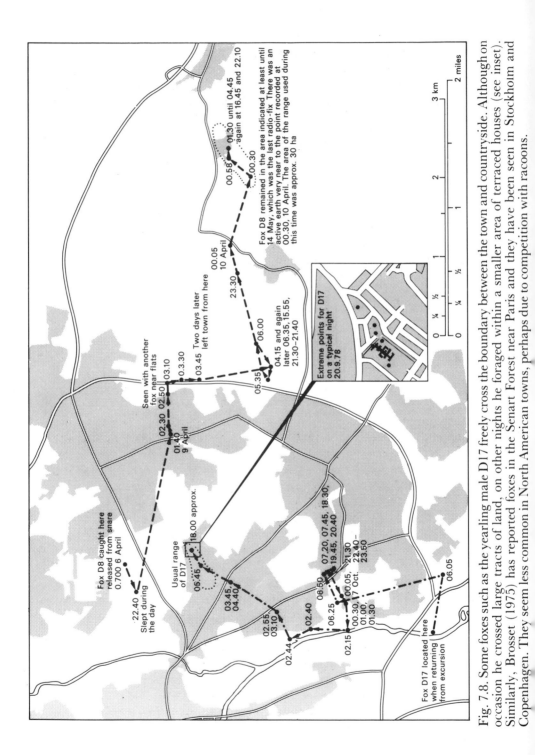

Fig. 7.8. Some foxes such as the yearling male D17 freely cross the boundary between the town and countryside. Although on occasion he crossed large tracts of land, on other nights he foraged within a smaller area of terraced houses (see inset). Similarly, Brosset (1975) has reported foxes in the Senart Forest near Paris and they have been seen in Stockholm and Copenhagen. They seem less common in North American towns, perhaps due to competition with racoons.

left the city bounday three nights later. At 03.15 on 9 April he reached the city by-pass and then travelled along the edge of the road (see the results of Thai Thien Nghia 1977, p. 75). The next day he slept in a wood on the outskirts of town, from whence he moved on to a village 1.5 km away by 00.04 a.m. He remained there for the next month (Fig. 7.8) (Macdonald and Newdick, unpublished data). Two other young males were followed on excursions from their probable birthplaces. One left the town, spent a night in the near-by farmland, and returned home by dawn. The second moved .5 km within the town, whence he made his way home over the next 48 h (Fig. 7.8). At 06.00 on the first night of his excursion this young dog fox was seen trying to cross a road in the direction of his home-range, but he 'lost his nerve' with traffic pressure and laid up for the day before continuing home the next night. A typical night's movements for this roughly 7-month-old fox is shown in the inset of Fig. 7.8 where his home-range can be seen to be within a very built-up area of terraced houses. The diet of these foxes is not fully known, but we have seen them carrying yoghurt pots and Kentucky Fried Chicken wrappers. Provisional results from the companion study in Bristol (Harris 1979) suggest a different pattern, with considerable overlap between some neighbouring ranges and little sign of territoriality. However, understanding the social biology of foxes in these two towns, with greatly differing fox densities, will take considerably more research. The complexity of the problem is illustrated by Hough's (1979) detailed longitudinal study of one vixen within our Oxford study area: as she matured the vixen left her natal range, traversed highly urban districts and established a series of temporary activity areas where she was seen with other foxes. Her relationships with these foxes and the factors underlying the pattern of her movements remain unknown (see Fig. 7.9).

So far research into fox biology has posed many more questions than it has answered. One might hope that in the foreseeable future it would be possible to look at the physical features of an area and predict from them the approximate population of foxes that the area might support and to know something about their behaviour. Such predictions are not beyond the realms of possibility. Newton, Marquiss, Weir, and Moss (1977) have been successful in predicting the density of sparrow-hawks in the UK from a map of soil fertility (an indirect indicator of prey numbers). As a provocative exercise I have attempted to guess the densities of adult foxes in the spring in different habitats in the UK based on what little is currently known about factors relating fox densities to habitat features. With the help of P. Bacon and R. Bunce I examined a sample of 256 maps of 1-km² areas on which habitats had been marked and classified according to a scheme described in Bunce

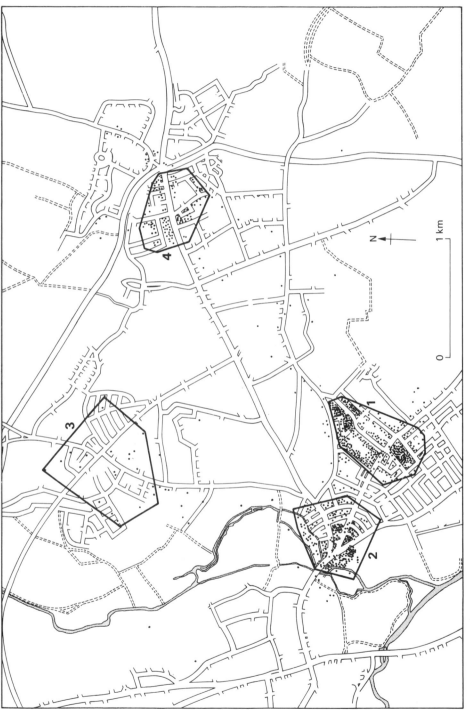

Fig. 7.9. Foxes have successfully colonized Oxford city. During a study of the behavioural ecology of these urban foxes we have found them in every habitat within the town. In this case a young vixen was born in area 1 (32 ha) where she was tracked from 18 September 1978 to 15 November 1978 apart from occasional excursions. Thereafter she moved successfully to area 2 (15 November to 30 November; 32 ha); area 3 (30 November to 5 December; 64 ha); and area 4 (5 December 1978 to 4 January 1979; 28 ha). During this time she was seen with other foxes, but the details of her social life remain a mystery. For clarity only the roads within the four temporary home-ranges and their vicinity are shown; a complete map of Oxford would

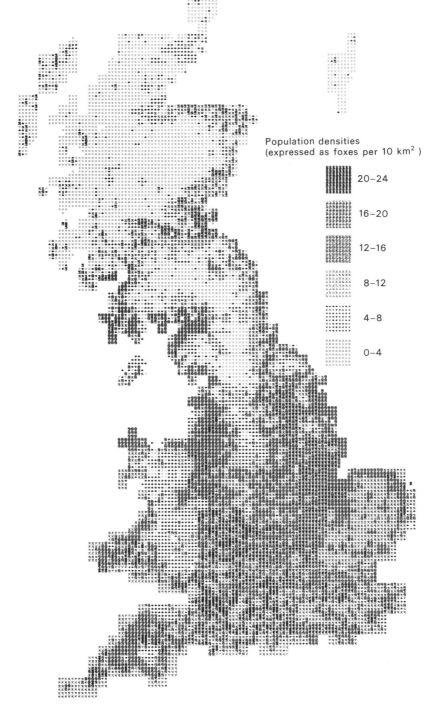

Population densities
(expressed as foxes per 10 km^2)

	20–24
	16–20
	12–16
	8–12
	4–8
	0–4

Fig. 7.10. A map of fox densities in spring based on guesses of the number of foxes supported in each of 256 sample habitat maps. Such a map could be vitally helpful in combating a rabies outbreak if it were moderately accurate. This map is not accurate; among the features I had to ignore was that some towns appear to have urban foxes and others do not — I had to base my estimates for all towns on the few samples for which we have data. Nevertheless, with further study it should be possible to resolve these problems. The map was drawn with the aid of P. Bacon and R. Bunce, and is reproduced with permission of the Institute of Terrestrial Ecology.

(1978). For each map I estimated the fox population which that habitat might support, and these figures have been used as the basis of extrapolation in order to draw a demographic map of fox numbers in the UK (Fig. 7.10). The map is probably wildly inaccurate (apart from everything else, it ignores any effects of local hunting pressures superimposed on habitat variables), but it does serve to illustrate the type of exercise which would be quite plausible on a more concrete footing if we knew more about the factors determining fox numbers and social organization. In fact, for places where I have worked the estimates based on map characteristics closely approximate estimates based on intensive radio-tracking and local knowledge in those areas. For instance, the map estimates for an area of Cumbrian fells was 0.251 adult resident foxes per km² while my 'observed' figure was 0.23, whereas lumping together all my Oxfordshire study areas (suburban and adjoining farmland) gave an estimate of 1.72 foxes per km² and an 'observed' of 2.15. Undoubtedly my estimates for habitat of which I have no direct experience will be far less reliable, but that is not a limitation of the method, only of my experience. In a search for an independent measure of this method it seemed that the number of foxes put up (but not necessarily hunted or killed) by packs of fox hounds during a day's hunting in different areas might hold promise as an index of relative fox abundance. At least the biases in using hound behaviour as an index seem rather more tractable than the biases of human motivation underlying normal hunting figures. A very preliminary analysis of data for the 1978–9 fox hunting season from 22 packs of foxhounds does show a significant ($p = 0.05$) linear correlation between the average numbers of foxes moved by hounds per day of the season and the average estimated population density of adult foxes per square kilometre of the hunts' territories.

On a wider scale H. Jackson (1979) has developed this approach further with P. Bacon and R. Bunce. Classifying European habitats on the basis of Bunce's system and comparing the resulting classification with areas of high or low incidence of rabies, they found that rabies occurred more frequently than expected in mosaic habitats, and less frequently than expected in homogeneous habitats such as arable regions and grassland. I have hypothesized (Macdonald 1977a) that patchily distributed prey supplies may favour the formation of groups, as opposed to pairs, of foxes. Whether or not this is true, it is almost certain that mosaic habitats will generally support more foxes than homogeneous ones.

The idea of using habitat classifications in this way is an exciting descendent of studies such as Kruuk's (p. 41) on hyaenas which demonstrated how mammal communities differ from one habitat to another.

However, the results reported here are so preliminary that it would be foolhardy to claim anything more for the technique than it deserves to be followed up.

In the preface to this book I described the control of rabies as being one of the most challenging problems to face wildlife biologists. It is exciting to be able to close with a report that may herald the solution to the problem. During early 1978 rabies spread fast in Switzerland, spreading to the bottom reaches of the Rhône valley by June. The epizootic spread through alpine passes at less than 1700 m, but rarely crossed passes of higher than 2000 m. On 17 October 1978 Alex Wandeler and Frans Steck (personal communication) distributed 400 chicken-head baits loaded with 10^7 I.U. of attenuated live vaccine (SAD ERA) (Steck *et al.* 1978). An area of 335 km² was covered with these baits at 12 baits /km². The baits were also marked with tetracycline. Rabies has disappeared from the area where vaccine was distributed and has not spread into the non-vaccinated upper part of the valley behind the vaccination barrier. Hence by vaccinating in a relatively small area a much larger area has been protected. Steck and Wandeler are naturally very cautious in interpreting their pioneering results and evaluation of the serology and tetracycline marking of more than 200 foxes killed in the area is still in progress, but even the most devout sceptic would acknowledge these results as encouraging. The risk, of course, is that live vaccine was used, and many authorities believe (see p. 117) that this is too dangerous and that large-scale oral vaccination must await the development of a suitable killed vaccine.

From the standpoint of rabies control it is important to persevere with fox studies in the UK, not only lest Britain ever has to face the disease, but also because those of us who work on foxes in Britain enjoy the privilege of studying under rabies-free conditions. Many data used in discussions of rabies control have been gathered from the disturbed areas where the disease is endemic and foxes are intensively hunted. An understanding of the social mechanisms of undisturbed fox communities may one day explain observations from populations decimated by rabies.

References

Acha, P. N. (1966). Rabies in the Americas. *Proceedings of the National Rabies Symposium*, pp. 140–3. CDC, Atlanta.
—— (1967). Epidemiology of paralytic bovine rabies and bat rabies. *Bull. Off. int. Epizoot*, **67**, (3–4), 343–82.
—— and Fernandes, N. (1976). Recent developments in endemic canine rabies. *Proceedings of the Symposium on Advances in Rabies Research*, p. 1. US Department of Health, Education, and Welfare, Atlanta.
Adamovich, U. L. (1974). Ecological evidence of the need for laboratory experiments into the foci of rabies in wild animals at low level population. *Bull. Moskovskogo Obshcetva I spytatelei Prirody Otdel Biologicheskii* **79** (6), 5–11.
—— (1978). Landscape–ecological prerequisites for the existence of natural foci of rabies infection. (In Russian.) *Zool. Zh.* **57** (2), 260–71.
Adams, D. B. and Baer, G. M. (1966). Cesariary section and artificial feeding device for suckling bats. *J. Mammal.* **47**, 524–5.
Andral, L. (1975). Quelques notions sur l'épidemiologie de la rage en France. *Symbiosis* **7**, 17–24.
—— and Joubert, L. (1975). Épidémiologie et prophalaxia écologiques de la rage. *Revue Méd. Mal. Infectieuses* **6**, 183–9.
—— and Roboly, A. (1977). Techniques de reduction de la population vulpine. In *La rage*, pp. 64–7, 113–23. Informations techniques des Services Vétérinaires.
—— and Toma, B. (1977). La rage en France en 1976. *Rec. Med. vet.* **153**, 503–8.
Aoki, F. Y., Tyrell, D. A. J., and Hill, L. E. (1974). Immunogenicity and acceptability of a human diploid-cell culture rabies vaccine in volunteers. *Lancet* **22**, March, 660–1.
Arambulo, P. U. and Escudero, S. H. (1971). Rabies in the Republic of the Philippines: its epidemiology, control, and eradication. *J. Philipp. Med. Ass.* **47**, 206–21.
Asferg, T., Jeppersen, J. L., and Sorenson, J. A. (1977). Graevlingen (*Meles meles*) og Graevdingojagen i Danmark, 1972/3. *Danske Vildtundersogelser* **28**, 56 pp.
Aubert, M. F. and Andral, L. (1975). Role éventuel des arthropodes dans l'épidémiologies de la rage. *Symbiosis* **VII** (1), 57–74.
Bacon, P. (1980). The consequences of unreported fox rabies (manuscript in preparation).
Baer, G. M. (1975). *The natural history of rabies*, Vols. I and II. Academic Press, New York.
——, Abelseth, M. F., and Debbie, J. G. (1970). Oral vaccination of foxes against rabies. *Am. J. Epidemiol.* **93**, 487–90.
——, Broderson, J. R., and Yeger, P. (1975). Determination of the site of oral rabies vaccination. *Am. J. Epidemiol.* **101**, 160–4.

—— and CLEARY, W. F. (1972). A model in mice for the pathogenesis and treatment of rabies. *J. infect. Dis.* **125**, 520–7.

——, LINHART, S. B., and DEAN, D. I. (1963). *Rabies vaccination of foxes: annual report of the division of Laboratories and Research*, New York State Department of Health, Albany.

BAILEY, N. T. J. (1975). *The mathematical theory of infectious diseases*. Griffin, London.

BAKER, E. F. (1967). N.L.D.L. zoonoses surveillance. *Annual rabies summary, 1968*, 8 pp. National Communicable Disease Centre, Atlanta.

—— (1978). Rabies in Europe and a comparison of European rabies data. *Publ. Hlth Reports* **93**, 186–8.

BARCLAY, P. S. (1958). *Practitioner* **181**, 626–33.

BARONOVSKYA, T. N. and KOLOSOV, A. M. (1935). Food habits of the fox (*Vulpes vulpes*). *Zool. Zh.* **14**, 523–50.

BELL, J. F. and MOORE, G. J. (1971). Susceptibility of carnivore to rabies virus administered orally. *Am. J. Epidemiol.* **93**, 176–82.

BERGER, J. (1976). Model of rabies control. In *Mathematical models in medicine, Lect. Notes Biomath.* **11**, 74–88.

BISSERU, B. (1972). *Rabies*. Heinemann, London.

BLACK, J. G. and LAWSON, K. F. (1973). Further studies of sylvatic rabies in the fox (*Vulpes vulpes*). Vaccination by the oral route. *Can. vet. J.* **14**, 206–11.

BÖGEL, K., ARATA, A., MOEGLE, H., and KNORPP, F. (1974). Recovery of reduced fox population under rabies control. *Zentbl. VetMed B* **21**, 401–12.

——, MOEGLE, H., KNORPP, F., ARATA, A., DIETZ, N., and DIETHELM, P. (1976). Characteristics of the spread of a wildlife rabies epidemic in Europe. *Bull. Wld. Hlth. Org.* **54**, 433–47.

BOTROS, A. M., MOCH, R. W., and KERKOR, M. E. (1976). Enzootic rabies in rodents in the Arab Republic of Egypt. In *Proceedings of the Symposium on advances in Rabies Research*, (1976), p. 3. US Dept. Health, Education, and Welfare, Atlanta.

BRAUNSCHWEIG, A. (1980). Ein Modell für die Fuchspopulationsdynamik in der Bundesrepublik Deutschland. In *The red fox: ecology and behaviour* (Proceedings of a symposium on fox biology, Saarbrucken 1979) (ed. E. Zimen). Junk, Den Haag. (In press.)

BROSSET, A. (1975). Régime alimentaire d'une population suburbain de renards au cours d'un cycle annuel. *La terre et la vie* **1**, 20–30.

BUNCE, R. G. H. (1978). An ecological survey of Cumbria. Working Paper No. 4. Cumbria County Council and Lake District Special Planning Board, Kendal, Lancs.

CONSTANTINE, D. G. (1966). Transmission experiments with bat rabies isolates. *Am. J. vet. Res.* **27** (116), 13–32.

—— (1967). *Rabies transmission by air in bat caves*. US Public Health Service Publication No. 1617.

—— (1971). Bat rabies: current knowledge and future research. In *Rabies*, (ed. Y. Nagano and F. M. Davenport), 253–62. University Parks Press, Baltimore.

——, SOLOMON, G. C., and WOODALL, D. E. (1968). Transmission experiments with bat rabies isolation: Responses of certain carnivores and rodents to rabies virus from few species of bats. *Am. J. vet. Res.* **29**, 181–90.

COREY, L. and HATTWICK, M. A. W. (1975). *J. Am. vet. med. Ass.* **21**, 232.

COSTY-BERGER, F. and MARCHAL, A. (1975). Recondescence de la rage animale en Belgique. *Annls. Méd. vet.* **119**, 241–53.

CRANDELL, R. A. (1975). Arctic fox rabies. In *The natural history of rabies*, Vol. II (ed. G. M. Baer), pp. 23–40. Academic Press, New York.

CRICK, J. and BROWN, F. (1976). Rabies vaccines for animals and man. *Vet. Rec.*, 28 Aug., pp. 6–11.

DEBBIE, J. G., ABELSETH, M. K., and BAER, G. M. (1972). The use of commercially available vaccines for the oral vaccination of foxes against rabies. *Am. J. Epidemiol.* **96**, 231–5.

——, BAER, G. M., ANDRALOUIS, J. A., SHADDOCK, J. H., and MOORE, S. A. (1979). Rabies vaccination of animals by the enteric route. (In press.)

ELLENTON, J. A. and JOHNSTON, D. H. (1975). Oral biomarkers of calcareous tissues in carnivores. *Proceedings of the Eastern Coyote Workshop*. Northeast Fish and Wildlife Conference, New Haven.

ELTON, C. (1931). Epidemics among sledge dogs in the Canadian Arctic and their relation to disease in arctic fox. *Can. J. Res.* 1931 **(5)**, 673–92.

ENGLUND, J. (1970). Some aspects of reproduction and mortality rates in Swedish foxes (*Vulpes vulpes*), 1961–63 and 1966–69. *Viltrevy* **8**, 1–82.

—— (1980). Population dynamics of the red fox (*Vulpes vulpes*) in Sweden. In *The red fox: ecology and behaviour* (Proceedings of a seminar on fox biology, Saarbrucken, 1979) (ed. E. Zimen). Junk, Den Haag. (In press.)

EVERARD, C. D. R., BAER, G. N., and JAMES, A. (1974). Epidemiology of mongoose rabies in Grenada. *J. wildl. Dis.* **10**, 190–6.

——, RACE, N. W., PRICE, J. L., and BAER, G. M. (1976). Recent epizoological findings in wildlife rabies in Grenada. *Proceedings of the Symposium on Advances in Rabies Research*, p. 8. US Department of Health, Education, and Welfare, Atlanta.

FAO (1966). *Survey of paralytic rabies in Latin America*, March 1966. FAO, Rome.

FENJE, P. (1960). A rabies vaccine from hamster kidney tissue culture: preparation and evaluation in animals. *Can. J. Microbiol.* **6**, 605.

FISCHMAN, H. R. and YOUNG, G. S. (1976). An association between the occurrence of fox rabies and the presence of caves. *Am. J. Epidemiol.* **104** (6), 593–601.

FLEMING, G. (1872). *Rabies and hydrophobia*. Chapman & Hall, London.

FREDERICKSON, L. E. and THOMAS, L. (1965). Relationship of fox rabies to caves. *Publ. Hlth Rep., Wash.* **80** (6), 495–500.

FRERICHS, R. K. and PRAWDA, J. (1975). A computed simulation model for the control of rabies in an urban area of Columbia. *Manag. Sci.* **22**, 411–21.

FRIEND, M. (1968). History and epidemiology of rabies in wildlife in New York. *Fish Game J, N.Y.* **15**, 71–97.

GARRIDO, R. (1978). *Rabies: the elimination of dog rabies in Malaga*. Report of Ministero de Sanidad y Seguridad Social, Spain.

GORDON SMITH, C. E. (1964). Factors in the transmission of virus infections from animals to man. *Scientific basis of medicine annual review*. Ch. VIII, 126–50.

GRANT, G. C. (1977). A simulation study of a red fox population with rabies. MA thesis. Queen's University, Ontario.

GRIBANOVA, L. Y., RUDAKOV , V. A., MAL'KOV , G. B., and SELIMOV, M. A. (1975). Results of ecological, virological and serological study of the natural foci of rabies in West Siberia. In *Problems of medical virology*. (In Russian.) Summary of the report of the xviiith review meeting of the Institute of Poliomyelitis and Virol Encephalitis, pp. 481–2. USSR Academy of Medical Science, Moscow.

HARRIS, S. (1977). Distribution, habitat utilisation and age structure of a suburban fox (*Vulpes vulpes*) population. *Mammal Rev.* **7**, 25–39.

—— (1978a). Age-related fertility and productivity in red foxes *Vulpes vulpes*, in suburban London. *J. Zool. Lond.* (In press.)

—— (1978b) Injuries to foxes (*Vulpes vulpes*) living in suburban London. *J. Zool., Lond.* **186**, 567–72.

—— (1979). Home ranges and patterns of distribution of foxes (*Vulpes vulpes*) in an urban area, as revealed by radio tracking. In *A handbook on biotelemetry and radio tracking* (eds. C. J. Amlaner, and D. W. Macdonald). Pergamon Press, Oxford.

HAVLIK, O. (1954). *Czech. Hyg. Epidem. Mikrobiol. Immunol. Prague* **3**, 300.

HELGASON, J. (ed.) (1960). *Öldin átjánda. Minnisverd tidindi 1701–1760*, p. 111. Forlagid Idunn, Reykjavik.

—— (ed.) (1961). *Öldin átjánda. Minnisverd tidindi 1761–1800*, p. 35. Forlagid Idunn, Reykjavik.

HENDERSON, G. N. and WHITE, K. (1978). *Rabies: the facts you need to know*, p. 145. Barrie and Jenkins, London.

HEWSON, R. and KOLB, H. H. (1973). Changes in the numbers and distribution of foxes (*Vulpes vulpes*) killed in Scotland from 1948–1970. *J. Zool., Lond.* **171**, 345–65.

HIRONS, G. J. M. (1977). A population study of the tawny owl, *Strix aluco*, L., and its main prey species in woodland. D.Phil. thesis, Oxford.

HOLE, N. H. (1969). Rabies and quarantine. *Nature, Lond.* **224**, 244–6.

HOUGH, N. G. (1979). Ranging behaviour of a maturing female red fox. In *A handbook on bioltelemetry and radio tracking* (ed. C. J. Amlaner jr. and D. W. Macdonald). Pergamon Press, Oxford.

INFORMATIONS TECHNIQUES DES SERVICES VÉTÉRINAIRES (1978). *La rage* (a collection of informative papers), **64–7**. Informations, Techniques des Services Vétérinaires, Paris.

JACKSON, H. C. (1979). A contribution to the study of fox rabies in relation to habitat in Europe. M.Sc. thesis, Imperial College, University of London.

JARMAN, P. J. (1974). Social organisation of antelope in relation to their ecology. *Behaviour* **58**, 215–67.

JENSEN, B. (1968). Preliminary results from the marking of foxes (*Vulpes vulpes*, L.) in Denmark, *Dansk Rev. Game Biol.* **5** (4), 3–8.

—— (1970). Effect of fox control programs on the bag of some other game species. *9th International Congress of Game Biologists, Moscow, 1969–70*, p. 480.

—— (1977). Raeven (*Vulpes vulpes*) og raevejagten i Danmark, 1973/4. *Danske Vildtundersogelser* **17**, 1–24.

—— and SEQUEIRA, D. M. (1978). The diet of the red fox (*Vulpes vulpes* L.) in Denmark. *Dan. Rev. Game Biol.* **10** (8), 1–16.

JOHNSTON, D. H. and BEAUREGARD, M. (1969). Rabies epidemiology in Ontario, *Bull. Wildl. Dis. Assoc.* **5**, 357–70.

—— and HRONCOCK, A. (1970). Abnormal feeding behaviour in red foxes naturally infected with rabies. Presented at the 1970 conference of the Wildlife Disease Association, National Communicable Disease Center, Atlanta, Georgia, USA.

—— and SARGEANT, A. S. (1977). *The impact of red fox predation on the sex ratio of prairie mallards.* US Department of International Fisheries and Wildlife Services Department **6**, 56 pp.

KANTOROVICH, R. A. (1957). The etiology of "Madness" in Polar animals. *Acta virol.* **1**, 220–8.

—— (1964). Natural foci of rabies-like infection in the far north. *J. Hyg., Epid., Micro Biol., and Immunol.* **8**, 100–10.

——, KONOVALOV, G. V., BUZINOV, I. A., and RIUTOVA, U. P. (1963). Experimental investigation into rage and rabies in polar foxes, natural hosts and infection. I. An experimental morphological study of rage in polar foxes. *Acta Virol.* **7**, 554–60.

KAPLAN, C. (ed.) (1977). *Rabies: the facts.* Oxford University Press

KAUKER, E. (1975). *Vorkommen und Verbreitung der Tollwut in Europa von 1966 bis 1974.* Seitzungsberichte der Heidelberger Akademie der Wissenschaften. Springer Verlag, Heidelberg.

—— and ZETTEL, K. (1960). Die Okologie der Rotfuchses und ihre Beziehung zur Tollwut. *Dtsch. Tierärgtl. Wrchr.* **67**, 463–7.

KONOVALOV, G. V., KANTOROVICH, R. A., BUZINOV, I. A., and RIUTOVA, V. P. (1965). Experimental investigations into rage and rabies in polar foxes, natural hosts of the infection. II. An experimental morphological study of rabies in polar foxes. *Acta Virol.* **9**, 235–9.

KOVALEV, N. A., SEDOV, V. A., SHASHENKO (1971). *Proceedings of the 19th World Veterinary Congress,* p. 113.

KRAL, J. (1969). Thumeni vztekliny. [Rabies control.] *Myslivost* **4**, 76–7.

KREBS, J. R. (1977). Song and territory in the great tit. In *Evolutionary ecology* (ed. C. M. Perrins, and B. Stonehouse). Macmillan, London.

KRUUK, H. (1972). *The spotted hyena.* A study of predation and social behaviour. University of Chicago Press, Chicago.

—— (1976). Functional aspects of social hunting in carnivores. In *Function and evolution in behaviour* (ed. G. Baerends, C. Baer and A. Manning), pp. 119–41. Oxford University Press.

LAMBINET, D., BOISVIEUX, J-F., MALLET, A., ARTOIS, M., and ANDRAL, A. (1978). Modèle mathématique de la propagation d'une épizootic de rage vulpine. *Rev. Epidém. et Santé Publ.* **26**, 9–28.

LAYNE, J. N. and McKEON, W. H. (1956). Some aspects of red fox and gray fox reproduction in New York. *Fish Game J, N.Y.* **3**, 44–74.

LEACH, C. N. and JOHNSON, H. N. (1940). Human rabies, with special reference to virus distribution and titre. *Am. J. trop. Med.* **20**, 334–40.

LEWIS, J. C. (1975). Control of rabies among terrestrial wildlife by population reduction. In *Natural history of rabies*, Vol. II (ed. G. M. Baer), pp. 243–57. Academic Press, New York.

LINDSTRÖM, E. (1980). The red fox in a small game community of the south Taiga region in Sweden. *The red fox: ecology and behaviour* (Proceedings of a symposium on fox biology, Saarbrucken, 1979 (ed. E. Zimen). Junk, Den Haag. (In press.)

LINHART, S. B. (1975). The biology and control of vampire bats. In *Natural history of rabies*, Vol. II (ed. G. M. Baer), pp. 221–41. Academic Press, New York.

——, FLORES CRESPO, R., and MITCHELL, S. C. (1972). *Bull. Of. Sanit. Panamer.* **73**, 100–9.

—— and KENNELLY, J. J. (1967). Fluorescent bone labelling of coyotes with dimethylchlortetracycline. *J. Wildl. Mgmt.* **31**, 317–21.

LLOYD, H. G. (1975). The red fox in Britain. In *The wild canids*, pp. 207–15 (ed. M. W. Fox), pp. 207–15. Van Nostrand Reinhold Co., NY, London.

—— (1976). Wildlife Rabies in Europe and the British Situation. *Trans. R. Soc. trop. Med. Hyg.* (Symposium on rabies) **70**, 175–203.

—— (1977). Wildlife rabies: prospects for Britain. In *Rabies: the facts* (ed. C. Kaplan), pp. 91–103. Oxford University Press.

—— and ENGLUND, J. (1973). The reproductive cycle of the red fox in Europe. *J. Reprod. Fert. Suppl.* **19**, 119–30.

——, JENSEN, B., VAN HAAFTEN, J. L., NIEWOLD, F. J., WANDELER, A., BOGEL, N., and ARATA, A. A. (1976). Annual turnover of fox populations in Europe. *Zbl. Vet. Med.* **B23**, 580–9.

MACDONALD, D. W. (1976). Food caching by red foxes and some other carnivores. *Z. Tierpsychol.* **42**, 170–85.

—— (1977a). The behavioural ecology of the red fox, *Vulpes vulpes*: a study of social organisation resource exploitation. D.Phil. thesis, Oxford.

—— (1977b). On food preference in the red fox. *Mammal Rev.* **7**, 7–23.

—— (1977c). The behavioural ecology of the red fox. In *Rabies, the facts* (ed. C. Kaplan), pp. 70–90. Oxford University Press.

—— (1978a). Radio-tracking: some applications and limitations. In *Recognition marking of animals in research* (ed. B. Stonehouse), pp. 192–204. Macmillan, London.

—— (1978b). I. The Sociable Fox, '78c. *Wildlife Mag.*, June.

—— (1978c). II. The Hungry Fox. *Wildlife Mag.*, July.

—— (1979a). Flexibility of the social organisation of the golden jackal, *Canis aureus*, *Behav. Ecol. Sociobiol.* **5**, 17–38.

—— (1979b). 'Helpers' in fox society. *Nature, Lond.* **282**, 69–71.

—— (1979c). Some observations and field experiments on the urine-marking behaviour of the red fox. *Z. Tierpsychol.* **51**, 1–22.

—— (1980). Social factors affecting reproduction by the red fox, *Vulpes vulpes*. In *The red fox: ecology and behaviour* (Proceedings of a symposium on fox biology, Saarbrucken, 1979) (ed. E. Zimen). Junk, Den Haag. Pp. 131–83.

—— and APPS, P. J. (1978). The social behaviour of a group of semi-dependent farm cats, *Felis catus*, a progress report. *Carnivore Genetics Newsl.* **7**, 256–67.

——, BALL, F., and HOUGH, N. G. (1979). The evaluation of home range size and configuration from radio-tracking data. In *A handbook on biotelemetry and radio-tracking* (eds. C. J. Amlaner jr. and D. W. Macdonald). Pergamon Press, Oxford.

—— and BOITANI, L. (1979). The management of carnivores: a plea for an ecological ethic. In *Animal rights* (ed. D. Patterson and R. Ryder). Centaur Press, London.

MacINNES, C. D. and JOHNSTON, D. H. (1975). Rabies control: experiments in behavioural engineering. *Ontario Fish & Wildl. Rev.* **14**, 17–20.

McLEAN, R. S. (1975). Raccoon rabies. In *The natural history of rabies*. Vol. II (ed. G. M. Baer), pp. 53–76. Academic Press, New York.

MANZ, D. (1975). Markierungsversuche an Fuchsen im Revier als Vorbereitung fur eine mögliche spätere perorale Vakzination gegen Tollwut. *Dtsh. Vet. Med. Ges., Bad Nauheim* **12** (4), 75.

MARTIN, R. J., SCHNURRENBERGER, P. R., and ROSE, N. J. (1969). Epidemiology of rabies vaccinations of persons in Illinois, 1967–68. *Publ. Hlth Rep., Wash.* **84**, 1069–77.

MAYR, A., KRAFT, H., JAEGER, D., and HAACKE, H. (1972). Orale immunisiering von Füchsen gegen Tollwut. *Zentbl. VetMed.* **B19**, 615–25.

MINISTRY OF AGRICULTURE, FISHERIES, AND FOOD (1977). Rabies memorandum by the MAFF and the DAF for Scotland.

MOEGLE, H., KNORPP, F., BÖGEL, K., ARATA, A., DIETZ, N., and DIETHELM, P. (1974). Zur Epidemiologie der Wildtiertollarut *Zentbl. VetMed. B* **21**, 647–59.

MOL, H. (1971). *Bull. Off. Int. Epizoot.* **75**, 808.

—— (1977). Rabies in animals as related to changes in the natural environment. *Przeglad Epidemiologczny* **31**, 195–205.

MOLLISON, D. (1977). Spatial contact models for ecological and epidemic spread. *J.R. Statist. Soc.* **B39**, 283–326.

MONTGOMERY, G. G. (1974). Communication in red fox dyads: a computed simulation study. *Smithson. Contrib. Zool.* **187**, 1–50.

MÜLLER, J. (1966). The reappearance of rabies in Denmark. *Bull. Off. int. Epizoot.* **65**, 21–9.

—— (1969). Rabies i Sonderjylland 1964–5. *Nord. Vet.-Med.* **21**, 65–80.

—— (1971). The effect of fox reduction on the occurrence of rabies. *Bull. Off. int. Epizoot.* **75**, 763–76.

—— and NIELSON, B. B. (1972). Rabies. Sonderjylland 1969–70. *Ward. Vet.-Med.* **24**, 203–16.

MURPHY, F. A. and BAUER, S. P. (1974). Early street rabies virus infection in striated muscle and later progression to the central nervous system. *Intervirology* **3**, 256–68.

MYASNIKOV, Y. A., LEVACHEVA, Z. A., and YOGIAZARYAN, K. K. (1961). *J. Microbiol. Epidemiol. and Immunobiol.* **32**, 815–24.

NAGANO, Y. and DAVENPORT, F. (ed.) (1971). *Rabies*. University Park Press, Baltimore.

NEWSOME, A. E., CORBETT, L. H. and STEPHENS, D. R. (1972). Assessment of an aerial baiting campaign against dingoes in central Australia. *CSIRO Div. Wildl. Res. Tech. paper* **24**, 11.

NEWTON, I., MARQUISS, M., WEIR, D. N., and Moss, B. (1977). Spacing of sparrowhawk nesting territories. *J. Anim.Ecol.* **46**, 425–41.

NIEWOLD, F. J. J. (1974). Irregular movements of the red (*Vulpes vulpes*) determined by radio-tracking. *XI International Congress of Game Biol. Stockholm*, 331–7.

—— (1976). Aspecten van het sociale leven van de vos. *Overdruk van Natura* **73** (9), 1–8.

—— (1977). *Het optreden van hondsdolheid in Nederlands sinds 1974*. Report to Rijksinstituut voor Natuurbeheer, Arnhem.

OFFICE OF HEALTH ECONOMICS (1976). *Rabies*. Office of Health Economics, Regent Street, London.

PARKER, R. L. (1975). Rabies in skunks. In *The natural history of rabies*, Vol. II (ed. G. M. Baer), pp. 41–50. Academic Press, New York.

—— and WILSNACK, R. E. (1966). Pathogenesis of skunk rabies virus. *Am. J.vet.Res.* **27**, 33–43.

PEARSON, D. P. and BASSETT, C. F. (1946). Certain aspects of reproduction in a herd of silver foxes. *Am. Nat.* **80**, 45–67.

PHILLIPS, R. L. (1970). Age ratios of Iowa foxes. *J. Wildl. Mgmt.* **34**, 52–6.

——, ANDREW, R. J., STORM, G. L., and BISHOP, R. A. (1972). Dispersal and mortality of red foxes. *J. Wildl. Mgmt.* **36**, 237–48.

PILS, C. M. and MARTEN, M. A. (1978). Population dynamics, predator–prey relationships and management of the red fox in Wisconsin. *Tech. Bull. No. 105*, Department of National Research, Wisconsin.

PIMENTEL, D. (1955). *Am. J.trop.Med. Hyg.* **4**, 147.

PRESTON, E. M. (1973). Computer simulated dynamics of a rabies-controlled fox population. *J. Wildl. Mgmt.* **37**, 501–12.

PRICE, J. L. and EVERARD, C. D. R. (1977). Rabies virus and antibody in bats in Grenada and Trinidad. *J. Wildl. Dis.* **13**, 131–4.

PRIOR, E. T. (1969). A study of rabies incidence in Western Virginia. M.Sc. thesis, Virginia Polytechnic Institute.

RAMSDEN, R. D. and JOHNSTON, D. H. (1975). Studies on the oral infectivity of rabies virus in Carnivora. *J. Wildl. Dis.* **11**, 318–24.

RAUSCH, R. (1958). Some observations on rabies in Alaska with special reference to wild canidae. *J. Wildl. Mgmt.* **22**, 246–60.

SARGEANT, A. B. (1972). Red fox spatial characteristics in relation to waterfowl predation. *J. Wildl. Mgmt.* **36** (2), 225–36.

SAYERS, B.McN., MANSOURIAN, B. G., PHAN TAN, T., and BOGAL, K. (1977). A pattern analysis study of a wild-life rabies epizootic. *Med. Inform.* **1**, 11–34.

SCHNURRENBERGER, P. R., MARTIN, R. J., MEERDINK, G. L., and ROSE, N. T. (1969). Epidemiology of human exposure to rabid animals in Illinois. *Publ. Hlth. Rep., Wash.* **84** (12), 1078–84.

SHOPE, R. E. and TIGNOR, G. H. (1971). Rabies and serologically related viruses from Africa. In *Rabies* (ed. Y. Nagano and F. M. Davenport). University Park Press, Baltimore, Md.

SIMMS, R. A., ALLEN, R., and SULKIN, S. E. (1963). Studies of the pathogenesis of rabies in insectionous bats III influence of the gravid state. *J. infect. Dis.* **112**, 17–27, Med. AN 86.

SMART, C. W. (1970). A computer model of wildlife rabies epizootics and an analysis of incidence patterns. M.Sc. thesis, Virginia Polytechnic Institute.

—— and GILES, R. H. (1973). A computer model of wildlife rabies epizootics and an analysis of incidence patterns. *Wildl. Dis.* **61**, 1–89.

SPITTLER, H. (1973). Zur Populations dynamik des Fuchses (*Vulpes vulpes*, L.) in Nordrhein-Westfalen. *11th International Congress of Game Biologists, Stockholm, Sept. 1973*, pp. 167–74.

STECK, F. (1975). Epidemiologische Bezimungen zarischen der Wildtaerund Maustiertollwut in Mittel Europe und derren Konsequenzen für die Bekämpfung. *Bundesgesundheitschdatt* **18**, 305.

——, HAFLIGER, U., STOCKER, CH., and WANDELER, A. I. (1978). Oral immunisation of foxes against rabies. *Experientia* **34**, 1662.

STEELE, J. H. (1973). The epidemiology and control of rabies. *Scand. J. Infect. Dis.* **5**, 299–312.

—— (1975) History of rabies. In *The natural history of rabies*, Vol. I (ed. G. M. Baer), pp. 1–29. Academic Press, New York.

STORM, G. L. (1965). Movements and activities of foxes as determined by radio tracking. *J. Wildl. Mgmt.* **29**, 1–13.

——, ANDREWS, R. D., PHILLIPS, R. L., BISHOP, R. A., SINEFF, D. B., and TESTER, J. R. (1976). Morphology, reproduction, dispersal and mortality of mid-western red fox populations. *Wildl. Mgmt.* **49**, 1–82.

STUBBE, M. and STUBBE, W. (1977). The population biology of the red fox, *Vulpes vulpes*. *Hercynia (NS)* **14** (2), 160–77.

SWINK, N. F. (1967). The role of the Bureau of Sport Fisheries and Wildlife in wildlife rabies control. Rabies Symposium, Frankfort, Kentucky. Cited in Prior (1969).

SYKES-ANDRAL, M. (1976). La rage du renard. Un danger méconnu: le renard en ragé. *Revue Méd. vét.* **127** (12), 1641–74.

TEAGLE, W. G. (1967). The fox in the London suburbs. *Lond. Nat.* **46**, 44–68.

THAI THIEN NGHIA, M. (1977). The implementation and use of statistical signal trend analysis for clinical and epidemiological medical data. Ph.D. thesis, Imperial College, University of London.

THOMPSON, R. D., MITCHELL, G. C., and BURNS, R. I. (1972). Vampire bat control by systemic treatment of livestock with an anticoagulant. *Science* **177**, 806–8.

TIERKEL, E. S. (1959). Rabies. In *Advances in veterinary sciences*, Vol. 5 (ed. C. A. Brandly and E. L. Jungherr), pp. 183–226. Academic Press, New York.

TOMA, B. and ANDRAL, L. (1977). Epidemiology of fox rabies. *Adv. in virus Res.* **21**, 1–36.

TRAUTMAN, C. G., FREDRICKSON, L. F., and CARTER, A. V. (1974). Relationship of red foxes and other predators to populations of ring-necked pheasants and other prey. South Dakota. *Trans. 39th N.Amer.Wildl.Nat.Res. Conf.* 241–52.

TURNER, G. S. (1977). Rabies vaccines and immunity to rabies. In *Rabies: the facts* (ed. C. Kaplan), pp. 104–13. Oxford University Press.

VERTS, B. J. (1967). *The biology of the striped skunk*. University of Illinois Press, Urbana.

—— and STORM, G. L. (1966). A local study of prevalence of rabies among foxes and striped skunks. *J. Wildl. Mgmt.* **30**, 419–21.

WACHENDÖRFER, G. (1976). Gegen wartiger Stand der Vakzionation von Fuchsen gegen Tollwut. *Praktische Tierarzt* **57**, 801–94.

—— (1977). *The problem of rabies in the European region.* 2nd European Conference on Surveillance and Control of Rabies, Frankfurt, November 1977.

—— and FÖRSTER, U. (1976). Safety testing of attenuated rabies vaccine in European wildlife species. *Proceedings of the Symposium on advances in Rabies Research (1976)*, p. 7. US Department of Health, Education, and Welfare, Atlanta.

WANDELER, A. (1976). Fox ecology in Central Europe in Relation to rabies control. *Proceedings of the Symposium on advances in Rabies Research (1976)*, p. 6. US Department of Health, Education, and Welfare, Atlanta.

—— (1976*b*). Altersbestimmung bei Füchsen. *Revue Suisse Zool.* **83**, 956–63.

——, WACHENDÖRFER, J., FÖRSTER, U., KREKEL, H., SCHALE, W., MULLER, J., and STECK, F. (1974*a*). Rabies in wild carnivores in Central Europe: I Epidemiological studies. *Zentbl. VetMed. B* **21**, 735–56.

——, ——, ——, ——, MULLER, J., and STECK, F. (1974*b*). Rabies in wild carnivores in Central Europe II: virological and serological examinations. *Zentbl. VetMed. B* **21**, 757–64.

——, MULLER, J., WACHENDÖRFER, G., SCHALE, W., FÖRSTER, U., and STECK, F. (1974*c*). Rabies and wild carnivores in central Europe: III ecology and biology of the fox in relation to control operations. *Zentbl. VetMed. B* **21**, 765–73.

WARRELL, D. A. (1977). Rabies in man. In *Rabies: the facts* (ed. C. Kaplan), pp. 32–52. Oxford University Press.

——, DAVIDSON, N., POPE, H. M., BAILIE, W. E., LAURIE, J. H., ORMEROD, L. D., KERTERZ, D. H., and LEWIS, P. (1976). Pathophysiologic studies in human rabies. *Am. J. Med.* **60**, 180–9.

WATERHOUSE REPORT (1971). *Report of the committee of inquiry on rabies*, Cmnd. 4696, HMSO, London.

WILLIAMS, R. B. (1969). Epizootic or rabies in interior Alaska 1945–67. *Can. J. comp. Med. B* **136**.

WINKLER, W. G. (1962). Rabies in the United States, 1951–1970. *J.infect. Dis.* **125**, 674–5.

—— (1976). Recent findings in oral rabies vaccination. *Proceedings of the Symposium on advances in Rabies Research (1976)*, p. 5. US Department of Health, Education, and Welfare, Atlanta.

—— and BAER, G. M. (1976). Rabies immunization of red foxes (*Vulpes fulva*) with vaccine in sausage baits. *Am. J. Epidemiol.* **103**, 408–15.

——, McLEAN, R. G., and COWART, J. C. (1975). Vaccination of foxes against rabies using ingested baits. *J. Wildl. Dis.* **11**, 382–8.

WORLD HEALTH ORGANIZATION (1979). *Rabies Bulletin in Europe.* WHO Collaborating Centre for Rabies Surveillance and Research, Tübingen.

ZINKE, G. (1804). Neue Ansiehten der Hundswuth, ihrer Ursachen und Folgen, nebst einer sichern Behandlungsart der von tollen Thieren gebissenen Menschen. *Gabler, Jena* **16**, 212. Cited in Steele (1975).

Author index

Subject index